Mother could not walk.

Wherever she went, Daddy had to carry her. And every Sunday, from the house to the car, from the car to the church, and back again, he carried her. And when Daddy would lay her back on her bed, Mother would smile, hold the sheet in her clenched fist, turn her head to the pillow—and close her eyes.

One day I came into the house and heard a sound I had heard only once before in my life—Mother was crying. As I listened she began talking to God in a strange prayer of desire—to be the wife her minister husband needed, the mother needed by a stumble-into-closed-doors little girl.

Some time later I heard the familiar sound of Daddy's key in the front door lock. "Myrtle? Chumper?" he called. "I'm home."

And I looked up to see Mother walking down the hall and into Daddy's arms!

I shall never underestimate the power of love.
I shall never underestimate the power of God.

The Most Important Thing

GINILOU DeMARCO

LIVING BOOKS
Tyndale House
Publishers, Inc.
Wheaton, Illinois

First printing, Living Books edition, May 1988

Library of Congress Catalog Card
Number 87-51337
ISBN 0-8423-4609-0
Copyright 1988 by Ginilou DeMarco
All rights reserved
Printed in the United States of America

The author and publisher express grateful
appreciation for permission to quote the following
copyrighted materials:

From "How Great Thou Art" by Stuart K. Hine.
Copyright 1953, 1955 by Manna Music, Inc., 2111
Kenmere Ave., Burbank, CA 91504. International
copyright secured. All rights reserved. Used by
permission.

From *Come Share the Being* by Bob Benson.
Copyright 1974 by Impact Books. All rights
reserved. Used by permission of The Benson
Company, Inc., Nashville.

To you who have left
sticky, indelible fingerprints
all over the fabric of my life

Special Thanks to:

God;

Mom—Myrtle Donaldson,
for typing, editing, and loving,
and loving, editing, and typing;

Dad—Dr. W. Albert Donaldson,
for listening to every word
and being my best audience;

Jayelynn, Stormi, Autumn Dawn—
for loving and pushing;

My closest friend—
for believing in me;

Randa Rottschafer—
for setting a goal and,
by ignoring all obstacles in the path,
birthing a dream;

Karen—
for using her editor's pen
with insight and friendship.

A special Thank You
to all who said I could do it—
and especially to all those
who said I could *not* do it!

In memory of
Betty Jones Allen
As long as the seasons work
their artful change on ancient trees
growing on the hills of Kentucky,
As long as cold water gurgles
over slate-bottomed creeks,
As long as I have breath in my body—
She is not gone.

Introduction

Psst!

Want to know what this book is about?

I'll tell ya!

It's about

love!

The most important thing there is—

love!

I want to whisper somethin' in your ear—just a quiet thought for you. Inside these pages you'll find me, and maybe you as viewed by me! I am forever haunted by the question that rings and echoes throughout my brain: "Do you have something to tell me?" Yes, indeed, I do! And this book is part of what I want to tell you.

What's this book about? It's my affirmation that love is forever a conscious, ongoing lifetime adventure; the most important thing there is.

"To everything there is a season,
    and a time to every purpose under
    heaven: . . .
    a time to weep, and
    a time to laugh;
    a time to mourn, and
    a time to dance" (Ecclesiastes 3:1, 4).
And now is the time to love!
The most important thing there is!

Departure Time—Orlando
7:00 P.M.

"If you swallow hard, your ears will pop and they won't hurt so much."

"Sir?"

"You were touching your ears. I assumed they hurt."

"They're OK now, thank you." I turned to look out the window and watched Orlando shrink to road-map size before my very eyes.

"Is this your first flight?" the man beside me spoke again.

"No, sir."

"You seem nervous. I thought perhaps it was."

"Do I? If I am, it has nothing to do with the flight."

"Sorry. Didn't mean to pry. My name is Rob Haywood."

"I'm Ginilou."

"With a 'J'?"

"With a 'G'. It's the *g-i-n-i* out of Virginia plus 'lou'—all in one word."

"Well, Ginilou with a 'G', what do you find so interesting out that window? You know, you just might give a person an inferiority complex real fast—you haven't even glanced in my direction!"

"Oh, I *am* sorry. It has nothing to do with you. I guess I'm just preoccupied with my own thoughts. But you're wrong, I did notice you when you boarded the plane."

"And what did you notice?"

"Well, let's see . . . I noticed that you walked down the aisle very sure-footedly as if you are used to flying. Everyone else came past me as if they were fourteen months old and wearing Pampers. You handed an expensive-looking briefcase to the flight attendant. You also touched her on the elbow as you passed her, so either you know her personally or you're accustomed to handling people. Your clothes are well-coordinated, shoes well-shined, haircut expensive. I'd guess that you have money. You're wearing a ring on your left hand but it isn't a wedding ring. *And*, judging from the questions you've asked, you're probably an attorney."

His laughter was warm, real, and infectious. People around us glanced over and smiled, and I found myself half-grinning back at this handsome stranger sitting beside me.

"Not bad," he said, "not bad at all. I do fly quite often. I am divorced. I am an attorney. But I do *not* know the flight attendant!"

"Oh, well, we just left the ground. With any luck at all you still have plenty of time to get acquainted with her before we land."

He chuckled and directed his attention to the

attendant as she walked away from us and down the aisle.

I turned my attention back to the clouds. Outside my window darkness had begun embroidering the edges of clouds with soft gray. In their center, the dying sunset colors shifted as fast as a child's rolling kaleidoscope, and night slowly zipped up her star-studded evening cape.

> O Lord my God!
> when I in awesome wonder
> Consider all the worlds
> Thy hands have made,
> I see the stars,
> I hear the rolling thunder,
> Thy power throughout
> the universe displayed:
> Then sings my soul
> My Savior God, to Thee;
> How great Thou art,
> how great Thou art!

What a magnificent ending for day!
What a fantastic beginning for night!
How much Mike would love to "see" a view like this one!

Mike had put himself through school, college, Juilliard School of Music, and one year had won a national award as Handicapped Man of the Year.

Mike was talented; he arranged music for well-known singers and musicians. Mike was black. And Mike was blind.

For a while we were both employed in the

same Community Relations Office. One day I overheard a visitor in Mike's office trying to describe the new office furniture to him.

"The desk," said the gentleman, "is mahogany. You do know what mahogany is, don't you, Mike?"

"No."

"Sure you do—mahogany, mahogany!" And the man got up in Mike's face and yelled the word louder and louder as if Mike were deaf, not blind.

Finally the insensitive soul left and I observed Mike just sitting there at his mahogany desk, drumming his fingers on the arms of his chair. I walked in and sat down.

"Mahogany . . . ," I said softly. "Mahogany. Mike, you've been on a farm?"

"Yes."

"You've smelled the heavy, rich, pungent odor of a sweating horse as he is rubbed down?"

"Yes."

"That's mahogany." And I got up and went back to my desk.

Shortly my telephone buzzed. I picked it up and heard Mike say, "Green. What's green?"

"Green . . . on a hot summer day, so hot you can scarcely breathe, perspiration drips from your hair across your face. It runs down your legs and into your shoes. You're so exhausted you feel as though you will drop, and there is, seemingly, no escape from the sun . . ."

"Yes," Mike said. "I've felt that way."

"Suddenly there is the cooling shade of a large tree and the sound of a small, gurgling, moving stream. You lie, belly down, on the earth under the tree, cup your hands beneath the flowing water, fill your hot, dry mouth with its life-restoring goodness and as you swallow—"

"Green," he said.

"Green," said I.

There seemed to be no end to the words Mike needed "Ginilou-descriptions" of. It became a large part of our association during the next few months.

Then one day at work, just an ordinary day, when we had no warning at all that our slice of the world was about to be turned upside down—

Shock.
Disbelief.
Martin Luther King, Jr.—
Assassinated!

Downtown offices and businesses closed early. Storekeepers boarded their doors and fled. Rumors spread faster than a raging fire. "There's going to be a riot. Get ready!" The men from the office went out on the street to see what was happening. The police force was out in full strength. Firemen stood ready.

I stayed in the office to answer the telephones and be the "go-between" for our office and the police department.

Then it was night. The streetlights blinked on in bewilderment, but someone decided that to keep them from being shot out, they should be turned off. And so the lights batted their bright eyes twice and went back to sleep.

Then the order came: "Extinguish all lights!"

Suddenly it was not only night, it was dark.

Dark, filled with strange sounds and muffled noises.

Dark, bigger than life and smothery with fear.

Dark, where the sound of your own swallowing is too loud.

Dark!

I heard the freight elevator start up and stop at my floor. The gates squeaked open. Someone was moving stealthily down the hall toward my office. I didn't move. I opened my mouth to breathe (because it seemed to me I could breathe more quietly that way). I couldn't see a thing! Not one thing. But I *knew* someone was there, moving toward me in the dark . . .

A hand touched my shoulder. "Come on, Sweetness, time to get you home."

"Mike? Oh, Mike!" I cried. "You scared me almost to death! Why didn't you speak? I had no idea it was you—I can't see a thing."

Mike just took my hand and held it easily as we walked away from my desk, out into the hall, and toward the elevator. I tried to match my unsure steps to his confident ones, and I held my left arm out in front of me so I wouldn't bump into anything.

Mike stopped suddenly and I felt him turn toward me. "Sh-h-h," he whispered. Then gently he disengaged his hand from mine. I heard a sudden movement and then there was nothing! Suddenly fear swept over me and I fought the hysteria I felt rising within me.

I reached out with both hands into the darkness just to touch something . . . but what? What might there be, waiting in the darkness for me to touch?

I wrapped my arms around myself and shivered. I felt tears of frustration running down my face.

"Blind," said Mike, from somewhere in the darkness. "Blind . . ."

Then his arm went around my shoulders and he took my hand again.

"Friend," he said softly as we moved off in the darkness, "friend."

Sometime much later realization set in: In "blind," "friend" has no color.

7:05 P.M.

"Ginilou, do you mind if we talk?"

"No, I don't mind."

"I dislike these flights that stop at every fencepost, but at least we don't have to change planes. Are you going to New York?"

"No, I'm going to Nashville."

"Oh, Music City, U.S.A. Going to the Grand Ole Opry, I'll bet."

"Wrong! I have an appointment with some people at a publishing house."

"For what purpose?"

"I wrote a book, and they say they like it. So I'm on my way to meet with them."

"I wish you luck."

"Thank you. I wish you luck too."

"Me? You wish *me* luck?"

"Yes, sir."

"Whatever for? Luck with what?"

"Whatever it is that is bothering you so."

"What makes you think I'm 'bothered so'?"

"Well, you sigh a lot, and make a snapping motion with your fingers, but there isn't any sound."

He turned his head away from me and stared across the aisle before motioning for the flight attendant. "Scotch on the rocks, please, my dear," he said, then turned back to me. "Oh, Ginilou, would you like one?"

"No, thank you."

"Do you object to my having one?"

"Would it make any difference if I did?"

"Absolutely none," he replied emphatically.

"Then enjoy your drink," I said.

"You sound like my psychiatrist!" he retorted.

He leaned back in his chair and gazed past me out the window. "Will you look at that sunset! It's breathtaking, isn't it? I always forget how beautiful Florida sunsets are."

"It's fantastic! God certainly has more beautiful colors in his paint set than I have in mine."

"Do you believe in God, Ginilou?"

"Yes."

"I don't know whether I believe in him or not. I've never been presented with spectacular enough, one-of-a-kind proof to really convince me of God's existence."

"I see. You believe in Law and Order?"

"Certainly. I have to. I see evidence of Law and Order every day. What's that got to do with believing in God?"

"I have to. I see evidence every day. As for a 'spectacular, one-of-a-kind' proof of God's existence, how about watching that spectacular, one-of-a-kind sunset?"

"Ginilou, was I the one who suggested we talk?"

"Yes, sir."

"Well, for the moment, I've changed my mind. I just want to drink my drink and look at the sunset. No more talk."

So we both settled back, him to his sunset and me to my thoughts about Nashville. *What will I find there?* I wondered. *I know only names that have no faces . . . oh, what if they don't like me in Nashville?*

I remember how it feels to be disliked. I wish I could forget—but I remember.

Twice a day I passed the iron fence. Once on the way to school and once on the way home. The fence was higher than my head and the gate was always closed and locked. The house squatted there, peering out of its shuttered windows at everyone who passed by. There was a big sign on one side of the gate that said "Beware of the Dog" and another on the other side that said "No Trespassing."

Twice a day, as I passed by, a large black dog charged the fence, growling and baring her teeth, making my knees shake and the blood pound loudly in my ears.

Twice a day I'd feel a strange fascination for that huge, black, velvet-coated animal with the sad brown eyes. I named her Velvet, and I did *not* cross to the opposite side of the street when I came to her fence like the other kids did . . . because I was the new kid in the fourth grade and I did not fit in.

I didn't have any friends.

I was scared and I began to stutter.

I much preferred Velvet's growling and snapping to walking on the other side of the street, alone in the middle of a bunch of kids who were laughing and jostling their way home from school.

Then one day I walked home a little more slowly 'cause I felt miserable about not knowing my fours in order. By the time I approached Velvet's fence, the other kids had long since vanished from sight.

I stopped at Velvet's gate and, taking a deep breath, pushed my sweating palms against the iron bars. I shut my eyes as Velvet charged and did not pull back till the weight of her body hit the fence.

"Velvet," I whispered, "Velvet, I am not afraid of you."

Velvet was not impressed. She growled and jumped higher than my head and showed me every tooth she had—every one—and when I wobbled away I saw her lick the fence where my hand had been.

After that I tried to walk home more slowly than the other kids.

Fall came and went and winter arrived and seemed to stay around forever. Every day I'd take off my hand-knit mittens and put my cold hands against the fence. When I'd walk away Velvet would stop her barking and sniff the fence. I don't remember when she exchanged her snarling and growling for barking at me, I only know that one day I noticed she had changed.

Spring finally showed small signs of dethroning Old Man Winter, and the remaining patches of snow and ice seemed to be waiting in line to slither down the sewer drain.

Then came the day I was not late coming home—I was early. Miss Killyan, my teacher, had sent me home.

We were asked to write a poem about spring and I did—and she said I copied it from somewhere, that I had cheated!

Only I hadn't!

The kids snickered while she pointed to the door and said, "Shame! Shame! Go home!" I wanted to cry, but I didn't. I just walked out the door holding onto my lunch bag with its half-eaten peanut butter sandwich, and clutching my "shameful" poem.

Velvet wasn't anywhere in sight when I reached her fence. I vaguely remember noticing that the gate was unlocked, so I reached up and opened it and walked down the long driveway toward the garage. Velvet watched me from her bed in a big box filled with straw, and she whined as I sat down beside her on the cold cement floor.

I scratched her ears and she proudly presented for my approval four tiny, black, velvet-coated puppies.

I nuzzled my head against hers and she pushed her muzzle against my hand. I cried and she licked my face clean. When the tears were done, I just settled in. Near as I can figure we all slept—Velvet, me, and four velveteen puppies.

I opened my eyes when Velvet growled and there stood a tall handsome man all in gray—

suit, shoes, eyes, hair, everything was gray. Even his face appeared gray and pale as he spoke in a too-soft voice.

"Little girl, don't move! I don't know who you are or how you got here, but I'll try to get you out safely. Now do not move."

Then he spoke sharply, "Come, Anastasia—come." But no one moved.

"Sir," I said, sitting upright and rubbing my eyes. "Sir, it's OK. Velvet and I are friends."

And Velvet thumped her stub of a tail affirmatively on the side of the box.

The man took a blanket out of the car and spread it on the floor. We sat there and talked and shared my half-eaten peanut butter sandwich.

He thought it was the best sandwich he had ever eaten. He didn't have any children to feed him peanut butter sandwiches. And he didn't have a wife. She had just disappeared one day.

He didn't like prying people, but he read my poem and he knew I didn't copy it. I gave it to him.

"To keep?" he asked.

"To keep," I said.

"It'll be a prized possession," he said, and I smiled.

Then it was no longer early, it was late. He walked me home and shook hands with my dad at the front door as I went inside. Daddy never asked why I was so late or how the teacher had liked my poem.

Velvet never growled at me again. The "No Trespassing" sign disappeared and the gates were no longer locked. My poem, encased in a fancy silver frame, lay on the marble coffee table in the elegant living room.

I was still the new kid in the fourth grade and I still did not fit in. But now I had a friend—and I stopped stuttering!

Oh, Nashville—
  Once again
  I am the new kid on the block but
  I am not afraid of you and
  I will not stutter.
  I only wonder—
  will I fit in?
  And will you be my friend?

7:15 P.M.

Rob spoke, interrupting my musing. "Ginilou, did I understand you correctly? You have written a book?"

"Yes."

"What's the title?"

"It's About Love."

"A book about love. Are you for it or against it?" he asked jokingly.

"Oh, I'm for it. Love beats a stick in the eye every time!"

"What kind of a book is it?"

"Well, it's a book about love, but it's not an everything-was-horrid-and-then-I-found-love-and-now-everything-is-peachy-keen book. It is not a boy-discovers-girl, hearts-and-Valentine book.

"It's a people-discovering-people book; a touch-your-heart, tear-in-your-eye, lump-in-your-throat, pat-on-the-backside book!

"It's about some of the people who walked down the halls of the doctor's office where I was employed for a few years. People who entered my life and touched me in such ways that I'll never be the same again.

"It's about my family, it's about pain, it's about discovery and daring to tear down the walls; being obstinate enough to defy the hurricanes of rejection and ridicule to fan a small inner flame of love."

Rob looked at me, his eyebrows arched high. "That's some book!"

"I hope so!" I said with a sigh.

The flight attendant interrupted our conversation to hand us a cup of coffee. As she left, I asked, "Are you from Florida or are you just vacationing?"

"Neither. I'm from New York. I was in Florida because of a client who is involved in a contested divorced action. The court awarded him temporary custody of his child, but a few weeks ago while he was at work, his ex-wife's parents came to his house and took his son. My client is sure that the boy's mother has him with her in Tampa. So I came down to check it out."

"Did you find him?"

"Sorry. I'm not free to discuss that part."

"I see. Why was the father awarded custody?"

"It's a long story. It isn't as if both parties live in the same state. The father is quite wealthy and can provide well for the boy, and the mother has nothing really."

"That's it? He has money and she doesn't?"

"No, of course that's not *it*. There are other

considerations . . . ," but Rob's voice trailed off and he made no attempt to mention what those other considerations were.

"Rob, why do you say the word *mother* as if you were saying *snake*, or *worm*, or *terminal acne?*" He looked at me, frowning slightly.

"I don't."

"Yes, you do."

Rob closed his eyes and moved his head against the back rest of his seat as if he were suddenly very tired. "I suppose you are going to tell me why," he said softly.

"Nope."

Rob opened his eyes and looked at me. "But you could guess."

"That's all it would be, purely a guess."

"Then do it—guess," and he spoke the words as though they were an order. He looked at me out of unblinking, steel-gray eyes, his jaw set defiantly and his right eyebrow slightly raised.

"Well," he demanded. "Go ahead!"

"Your mother," I said, taking a deep breath, "died, or walked out, when you were a small child."

His left eyebrow joined his right one for a second. "Yes, walked out, left, deserted. How did you know?"

"I didn't know."

"Yes, you did! How did you know?"

"I've seen that look before."

"Before?"

"Yes. Did you think you were the only one?"

"I . . . I . . . no, I know I'm not the only one. But you *know* someone . . . a . . . some . . . whose . . . ," and he rubbed his hand across his face and left his uncompleted thought just floating there on the air between us.

"Yes, I know someone," I said gently.

Rob moved around a bit in his seat as if to find a more comfortable position before speaking again. "I don't even think about it anymore. I mean, I used to think about it a lot when I was a kid, but I never think of it anymore.

"I was six when she walked out. She took my brother and me to a neighbor's house and said that she'd be back in an hour or so—and that was the last we ever saw of her.

"Dad raised us by himself. He lives in Louisville now, my brother Joe lives in Los Angeles. I'm in New York and I just never think of it anymore."

"I see."

"But you don't believe me?"

"Whether I believe you or not doesn't matter, Rob, as long as *you* believe it."

"You're probably one of those people who thinks all my relationships with women are affected by that one incident, aren't you?"

"Do you think so?"

"I told you, I don't think about it at all."

"Right. You did tell me that."

"It wasn't easy for Dad rearing two boys alone. It wasn't easy for Joey and me, either."

"I am sure that it wasn't."

"You have no idea."

"Probably not. But perhaps my three girls could identify with you somewhat."

"I really don't want to talk about it anymore."

"Right."

"Three girls?"

"Yes."

"They live with you?"

"Yes."

"Its really tough on boys who grow up without a mother. I never thought much about girls growing up without a father."

"I have."

After a silence of considerable length, Rob cleared his throat. "Dad never talked to us much about . . . about . . ."

"Your mother?"

"Yes. *Her.*"

"It really isn't all that difficult a word to say. Try it. Just make an *mmmmmm* sound: 'Mmmmmm' plus *other*—'mother'! See?"

"Yes, I see. Your sarcasm has been duly noted! Anyway, he never said much about her. But the summer I graduated from law school he took me camping in Colorado. One night he just seemed to *have* to talk about her. He kept saying over and over how much he regretted that he hadn't paid enough attention to her, hadn't seen it coming. He was so sure that if he had been observant, he could have done something."

"Maybe. Maybe not. Sometimes things happen that we aren't aware of—things that are completely beyond our comprehension, even if we are observant."

"But he was a good man. He *is* a good man."

"Does the idea bother you that perhaps, just perhaps, she was—and is—a good woman?"

"Yes! That idea is totally unacceptable! Just

what could have happened that was so important? Nothing! Nothing could have been so important that she would just walk out like that—no explanation, no nothing."

"Sometimes, Rob, we just never know. Things happen practically everyday, just out of our line of awareness, to the people in our own personal world. Things that are beyond our scope and that we are completely unable to change. Things that have the potential to alter our lives forever."

More than twenty-five years ago, he walked into my life, and things seemed to me to be progressing at a normal pace and heading in a predictable direction. Then, from out of a "where" I could not see and a "what" I did not know— Shazam!

Johnny was the kind of boy that every girl immediately knows she can take home to meet her parents and they'll approve.

Johnny was the kind of boy that every girl immediately wants to take home—whether or not her parents ever approve.

Johnny was the kind of boy every girl immediately wants.

Why Johnny paid attention to me, I'll never understand. But he did. And we were, in the eyes of observers, "charmed."

Johnny was an engineer at one of the local radio stations, and it so happened that one Sunday morning he was sent to our church to do a "pick-up" broadcast of the morning service. I was the vocalist that morning. That's how we met.

That afternoon he called me and asked me to go out, and so it all began.

There was lots of
    laughter
  and hand holding,
     practical jokes
     and kissing,
    telephone conversations
      that never lasted long enough
      no matter how long they lasted,
   letters (when we were apart)
     that never said enough
     no matter how much they said.

He made lots of tapes of my singing and playing, and once he gave me a record that he had made especially for me—of me.

He always called me "Monkey,"
  and I never asked him why.
The months passed and there were
    football games
      and car rides,
    basketball games
      and long walks,
    baseball games
      and picnics,
  and lots of hand holding
    and kissing.

Then one Saturday evening he called unexpectedly and asked if he could come and take me for a drive. "Because," he said. "Because I have to see you tonight. It's important!"

I showered and dressed hurriedly. As I brushed my hair I looked in the mirror and wondered why Johnny's voice had not sounded as usual on the telephone—not quite so carefree, not quite so happy.

Before I could give it much thought, I heard him downstairs in the living room talking to my dad. I put on some lipstick and a dab of perfume and rushed down to meet him.

We got in the car and drove off. He reached over and held my hand, and I moved closer to him. He turned on the radio and as we drove we listened to the music. He apparently didn't want to talk, so we didn't.

At eight o'clock the radio announcer said, "We're playing this next music for Monkey. Have a good evening, Monkey. This is especially for you."

"Johnny, thank you."

"Don't thank me."

"Why not?"

"Just don't. Listen to the music."

He drove to a point high above the city and we sat there in the dark with his arms around me. We listened to the music and watched the lights of the city.

"Monkey, my dear sweet Monkey," he said and ran his fingers through my hair and traced my lips with his fingertips.

I could not understand the sadness about his eyes. They usually twinkled and shone with an inner sparkle that had never seemed to dim—until now.

"Johnny, is something wrong?"

"Sh-h-h-h. Sh-h-h-h," he whispered sadly.

Later, much later, he drove me home. At the door he would not look into my eyes. He only said, "When you get to bed, turn on the radio and listen to the station's music at 11:15."

I turned, opened the door and stepped inside. I was still wondering just what had been so terribly important that he had had to see me about.

He walked down the steps, and as I closed the door I heard him say, "Monkey, please—please, wait a minute."

I stepped back onto the porch and he held me as though he could not let go, rubbing his face against my neck. He kissed me gently. "Good-bye, Monkey."

And then he let me go.

I went to bed and listened to the radio in the dark. At 11:15 the announcer said, "Pleasant dreams, Monkey, this is for you, especially you." The first song was "My Funny Valentine." In the back of my head I kept wondering about those words, "Good-bye, Monkey." Not "Good night" ... Good-bye?

Sunday morning came, and as I stood in the choir room at the church putting on my robe, the choir director came over and patted my hand as if I were terminally ill and didn't know it.

"Ginilou," he said, "how do feel?"

"OK, Professor."

"Are you sure? You're really OK?"

"Sure. Why?"

"Ginilou, you haven't seen the morning paper, have you?"

"No, why? What's in the morning paper?"

But he looked over the top of my head as if I were no longer visible. "OK, choir," he said, "time to get going."

When the service was over I rushed home and went straight for the morning paper, not knowing what I was looking for. I found it anyway! There it was, in letters black and bold:

Sunday morning—
This very Sunday morning—
at 10:30 A.M.
Johnny—
Johnny, the pal,
Johnny, the true,
Johnny, the charmed
and
Miss Something-or-other,
wearing white lace and a pearl tiara,
were married
before God
and a church of well-wishers.

I carefully refolded the paper, picked up the telephone, and dialed the radio station. There was no office staff on Sunday, but finally the announcer answered the telephone from the control booth.

"This is Ginilou," I said quietly.

There was a long, long pause. Finally, in a pained voice, he said, "He didn't tell you, did he?"

"Just tell him," I said in measured tones, "tell him that I called and that I said good-bye."

"Ginilou," Mother called from the kitchen, "time to set the dinner table."

I hung up the telephone, ending the inane, inadequate, well-meaning words I did not want to hear.

"Coming, Mother."

Good-bye, Johnny, good-bye.

7:20 P.M.

"You know," Rob said, "now that I think about it, either way—boys without mothers or girls without fathers—no matter which way, it still comes up minus."

"I'm sure that's true," I agreed. "It seems when you're minus a parent, no matter how many grandparents you have, or uncles and aunts, or well-meaning 'substitute' mothers and fathers, all of 'em added together still wouldn't total enough.

"In one of my favorite books, *Come Share the Being* by Bob Benson, he speaks of the time when he and his wife, Peg, emotionally deposited their oldest son at college."

Oh our hearts were filled with pride
at a fine young man,
and our minds were filled with memories
from tricycles to commencements;
but deep down inside somewhere
we just ached with loneliness and pain.

Somebody said you still have three at home,
three fine kids—and there is
still plenty of noise—
plenty of ball games to go to,
plenty of responsibilities,
plenty of laughter,
plenty of everything . . .
except Mike.
And in parental math,
five minus one
just doesn't equal plenty.

"No matter how 'well-meaning,' " Rob said
sadly, "it seems that good intentions never quite
make it. Good intentions or not, their words
hurt. I remember overhearing the adults talking
when Joey and I were little. 'Now let's invite Rob
and Joey over—you know how hard it must be
on their father,' they'd say. 'Rob and Joey don't
know about closing the bathroom door. After all,
there're just the three men'; 'Rob and Joey
wouldn't know about *those* days and women.
Ha-ha-ha.'

"You hear a lot about the cruelty of children,
but adults don't understand that they are no less
cruel just because they are smiling while they're
saying the words."

"I know," I said, nodding.

"As I look back, it seems to me that the adults
had no words to help me with my pain. All they
ever did was pat me on the head or buy me an
ice cream cone as if they thought that helped."
He turned his head to hide the pain in his eyes.

"It's a shame that some adults fail to realize

that a two-and-a-half-foot body filled with hurt
and sorrow is no less painful than a six-foot
body filled with heartache."

The scooter was bright red and it belonged to
Ronnie. Sometimes he would ride it around the
block. Sometimes I would. And sometimes we
both would. It wasn't a question of taking turns
or being nice. Grown-ups just never did understand that.

It was just that sometimes Ronnie felt like
riding by himself.
And sometimes I wanted to be by myself and
pretend
I was rushing off to something
terribly, terrifically important.
Or I was in this race, you see,
and I was the first girl *ever* to ride
in this race—
and all the people I knew in the
whole wide world
were all lined up around the block
to cheer for me,
'cause I was going to win
'n everybody would be proud of me—
'n I'd be a hero, or somethin', you see?

Sometimes Ronnie would have me stand at the
front of the scooter with my feet tight together.
He would put his hands on the black handlebar
grips (which always stuck to your fingers and
left horrid marks on the bathroom towels,
driving Mother straight up the wall), and I'd put

my hands on top of his. He'd push off and away we'd go—kinda wobbly at first, then straightening out as we picked up speed. The wind would whip my hair and stick it tight to my face. I'd feel the jolt as we'd cross each crack in the sidewalk.

At each corner Ronnie would yell, "Hold on!" and as we would lean to one side, I'd feel like we were falling and I'd shut my eyes and want to scream or jump off. But I wouldn't dare! I'd just turn my head and push it back against Ronnie's shoulder, and he'd laugh at my being scared, "Jus' like a girl!"

The grown-ups would watch and smile and say, "It's a shame she doesn't have a scooter of her own. They have so much fun together. Aren't they sweet? Isn't it nice the way they share?"

It was summer and we were children.
And it would never be like that again.
    For winter came
    with her snow and sleds and slippery streets,
    and drivers who drank too much
    and didn't notice small boys
    sledding home at dusk.
And the room smelled too sweet.
    There were too many bright flowers
    and not even one small violet
    like we used to pick in summer
    from under the rocks
    on the side of the hill.
They gave me his red scooter.
They never understood.
    I didn't like that ole scooter anymore—
    I never rode a scooter again.
    It was not a question of being nice.

It's just that
   I didn't need
      a scooter
        all my very own.

7:25 P.M.

Rob shifted his position, stretched his arms above his head, and yawned, "I'm curious, Ginilou, what made you write a book?"

"There is no simple answer to that question. I moved to Florida mostly as a means of 'escaping' after my divorce. I fled there as to a refuge. And because of my baby girl, Autumn Dawn. It was extremely important to me that she have a strong, loving male figure in her young life, and the most loving man I know is my dad, who lived in Florida. So we moved there, my three girls and I. And it has been good for us to have the closeness and love provided by my parents.

"One day an acquaintance, the Reverend Bill Giesler, looked me up and asked me to become the organist at the church where he pastored. So I agreed.

"I found Bill to be much as I remembered him—God's man, an interesting speaker, caring and supportive of people.

"I found the church to be like any other group of people. There were wondrous people there and there were children of the devil. There were times of great joy and times of jealousy and hate; times of warm acceptance and times of painful rejection; times of truth and times of half-truth (more destructive than outright lies); times of rejoicing and times of crucifying.

"Then one Sunday morning, I looked out over the congregation, into each face and each pair of eyes. With very few exceptions the faces were cold and hard. Some were bitter, some were even unfeeling or evil. Most of them appeared to be carved out of stone. There didn't seem to be enough love there to light a candle.

"Later, at home, shivering under the covers on my bed, I cried out, 'O God! Don't let me become that unfeeling. Open my heart—please, let me feel again. Let love flow through me. Don't allow me to become stone. Fill me, every nook 'n cranny, every pore, with love.' "

"And did he?" Rob asked.

"Nope. Not at first. He couldn't! I had kept areas of my life devoid of feeling anything—especially love—for too long. In essence, I had carefully made out a list of persons who were safe to love: my parents, my kids, sick people, little children, God . . . and that's about all! But I would not allow any other 'love'—not friendship love, not romantic love—to get in.

"You know, one of God's greatest miracles is romantic love. But when you've been hurt enough and when you're positive that there is no such thing for you, you build a wall. But the wall not only keeps you from discovering that special love, it also becomes so confining that it hampers your ability to feel love of *any* kind.

"So, to answer your question as to why I wrote a book, it was partially to tell people not to build walls to keep out love."

"Miracle of love . . . ," he said softly, as if musing to himself.

"I beg your pardon?"

"Miracle of love . . . you said that one of God's greatest miracles of love is romantic love. Do you really believe that love is a miracle?"

"Yes, I do! It has everything going against it, and still it happens!

"This is a fast-paced world where everything is geared for s-p-e-e-d and hurry up—where you have to get somewhere, be somebody, be first by push and shove—where it's only number one that counts and to heck with the other guy! If, in such a world, two pairs of eyes meet and two hearts skip a beat, we won't count on its meaning a great deal because we're all caught up in the 'one-night stand' syndrome!

"Yes, I do believe that love is a miracle. In fact, it's not only a miracle—it's the greatest force that I know anything about. Rob, don't ever underestimate the power of love."

For as long as I can remember, whenever it is time for a serious talk with Daddy, I perch on the end of his desk and he sits in his chair. Sometimes I understand and sometimes I don't.

Sometimes he understands and sometimes he doesn't. But we always care enough to try, and somehow that helps.

When I was eight years old there were words I did not understand until much later:

"Tomorrow," he said, "tomorrow I will bring Mother home from the hospital—but she will not be able to walk."

And it was so!

Over the days, weeks, and months, I began to understand. Other kids' mothers could walk. Mine could not.

Wherever Mother went, Daddy had to carry her. And every Sunday . . .

From the house
    to the car;
From the car—up the stairs—
    into the church;
From the church—down the stairs—
    to the car;
From the car
    into the house,
        down the long hall,
        into the bedroom, and
        over to the bed.
    Mother smiled,
    held the sheet
    in her clenched fist,
    turned her head
    on the pillow—
    and closed her eyes.
Mother could not walk.

Then one day school let out early and, for some unknown reason, I came into the house quietly. (I have never done anything quietly.) I came into the hallway and heard a sound that I had heard only once before in my life—Mother was crying.

So I sat myself down in the hallway outside Mother's bedroom door and leaned against the wall. As I listened, she began talking to God.

It was a strange prayer of desire—to be the wife that her minister husband needed, the mother needed by a stumble-into-closed-doors little girl. It was a strange prayer of acceptance . . . of love. And I will never tell exactly what she said, for that would be like touching the petals of a gardenia and watching them turn brown.

And so I sat, and listened. And in the ever-lengthening shadows gathering in the hallway, sleep settled over me.

Sometime later, from somewhere deep in my dreams, I heard the familiar sound of Daddy's key in the front door lock. I pulled myself upright and rubbed at my sleep-filled eyes with both fists.

"Myrtle? Chumper?" Daddy called from the front door. "I'm home!"

And Mother *walked*
    down the hall—
    and into Daddy's arms!
I shall never underestimate the power of love.
I shall never underestimate the power of God.

7:35 P.M.

"I suppose," Rob said, "one of the reasons I am feeling a bit on edge is that tonight would have been our twenty-fifth wedding anniversary. Wouldn't you think I ought to feel sad or something?"

"What do you feel?"

"I don't know. I've been sitting here trying to figure that out . . . mostly relieved, I think."

"You didn't love her?"

"I used to say I did when I was pushed into saying it. I know that I felt affection for her—I still do—I suppose that's a *kind* of love. We were 'comfortable' together and there was a closeness of a type that comes from living together and sharing life for some twenty years. But even I know that what I've just said doesn't answer your question. No, I really didn't love her. You know, I'm not all that sure that I'd really know what true love feels like!"

"You'll know it, when it happens—if you allow it to happen."

"And you, Ginilou, when you fall in love again how will you know it?"

"My knees will smile."

His laughter exploded and bounced from seat to seat up and down the aisle throughout the airplane. People about us looked at one another and grinned at something they didn't understand.

"And have your knees *ever* smiled?" he asked.

"Boy, howdy! Uh-huh!"

He lived next door to my grandparents in Hamilton, Ohio. He was a show-off, the way little boys are apt to be. He seemed so tall (he must have been almost five feet tall) and so brave (he could ride his bike down the sidewalk and out Mr. Peterson's driveway into the street and never even touch the handlebars!). He used to swagger down the street and yell at us three girls playing on the front porch. There was Janie with her lisp and hair over one eye; and Susan with her pout and loud laugh; and me with—whatever it was I had. A motley crew if ever there was one.

One afternoon he ran past me and pushed a note into my hand. I walked into the backyard and sat under the grape arbor to read it.

"I love you."

Maybe not an original, but a first for me.

Grass was cool under the grape arbor and I lay there—still, scarcely breathing, feeling the smile creep across my face and wondering a bit at the feeling of bubbles in my tummy. I held the moment close so as never to forget what it first feels like to wonder at being a girl.

But there were things to be done—
set the table;
wash the hulls off the beans soaking in the
    pan,
their little wrinkled bodies clinging to my
fingers like leeches.
There was supper
and a bath,
with the bath salts making a squeaky squish
as I stepped on them in the slightly too-hot
    water.
There was combed hair and a clean dress—
and then it was evening, complete with a
    katydid chorus.
We met at the back fence.

He walked along on his side of the fence and I walked along on my side.

"Didja like it?"

"What?"

"My note. Didja like it?"

"It was very nice."

"A . . . a . . . a . . . can I come over and sit in your front yard?"

"Yes."

We sat on the grass under the trees and tried to ignore the little nudges and smiles of the grown-ups on the front porch. The air was cool and the smell of roses was very much like the odor left by the bottle of perfume I had spilled on Mother's dresser and tried to clean up with a Kleenex and a white sock.

Finally he said, "Do you?"

"Do I what?"

"You know."

"What?"

"Well," he said, "I do, an' I'm going to marry you." With that he was gone, jumping the fence and whistling as he ran up the street.

The mosquitoes buzzed 'round and Granny mumbled, "That child will be eaten alive by them bugs if you all don't get her in here."

Somebody giggled and said, "Isn't puppy love grand?"

The swing squeaked its hesitant tone; the porch screen slammed; the lights began winking on in the house. Someone sighed.

Granddaddy said, "Aw, let her alone—she'll be in, in a minute."

That night I sat on the bed in Granny's guest bedroom and with my very first blue Sheaffer fountain pen that Daddy brought to me from New Kensington, I drew round eyes and a lazy smile across my tickly knee!

That was years ago when I was but a child. No longer do I draw on my knees with a fountain pen. But, ah! Wish I could feel that way again!

"Oh Ginilou, someday there will be a girl whose knees will smile because of me!"

"Right!"

"Do you know, when I think of love I find myself remembering clear back to my third-grade teacher, Miss Lauren. What a woman she was! She never laughed at me, though she must have been terribly embarrassed by my case of puppy love."

"No such thing as puppy love."

"No?"

"No, not that I know of. That term has always made me so mad.

"When Autumn Dawn was five-years-old, she was in love with Ray, who is in his twenties. She loves him to distraction, and if he lives to 492 he will never be loved more than he is loved right now by her. She loves him completely, to her total capacity for loving.

"I may have a greater capacity for and under-standing of love (maybe not), but I'll never be able to give more than my all. That is what she gives at five—all her love."

"Are you telling me that I can stop being embarrassed every time I remember Miss Lauren?"

"You loved her. That's all."

"Yes I did. And I remember how that love felt. I'd give a whole lot just to feel like that again!"

7:45 P.M.

"Ginilou, are you asleep?"

"No."

"Do you believe that every man has a destiny to fulfill? I mean, churches speak of a 'calling,' don't they? Sort of a special reason for being? Do you understand my question?"

"I think so. And, yes, I believe everyone has a 'destiny,' a 'calling,' a 'ministry' to fulfill. I also believe he may choose to ignore it."

"Then you believe you have a . . . a . . . what-ever?"

"Yes."

"What is it?"

"To use the talents God gave me to the best of my ability.

To touch
with words written and sung.
To listen
with the ear and
the heart.

To stir the heart
   because we are in great danger
   of letting it die
   if we forget
   to let it feel."

"I wish," Rob mused, "I could sense some purpose to my life—some higher, nobler feeling than I have most of the time.

"It would be nice if people took the time really to see each other and genuinely to care for each other. Instead, we go around stepping on anyone who gets in our way.

"Tell me, Ginilou, do you talk to God?"

"Yes."

"What do you say?"

"Whatever I want to say."

"I wouldn't even know how to begin. I'd be afraid I'd use the wrong terminology."

"You sound as if you're composing a legal brief. For me, prayer is sometimes just thought— no formal phrases. Sometimes, it's not even audible wordage.

"I don't have to be on my knees at bedtime. Prayer is not necessarily 'O Most Gracious Lord, I come before thee to thank thee for thy most bounteous blessings bestowed upon me.' Usually, for me, it's more like, 'Hey, thanks heaps.' "

"He understands that?"

"He does. He made me the way I am. He knows me inside out, through and through. I may try to snow you, but I wouldn't dare try to snow him. Near as I can tell, he has always been straight with me—no games. I like it that way."

"Anytime I've ever heard anyone pray," Rob

said, "I knew immediately that they were praying by the tone of their voices and all of those 'thees' and 'thous.' "

"You ought to meet Bill Eddy, a pastor in Kenosha, Wisconsin. He's the husband of one of my best pals, Ruby. There have been times when Bill and I have been talking on the telephone when he has included God directly in our conversation. He hasn't preceded it by saying, 'Let's have a word of prayer.' His voice doesn't drop three octaves in mid-sentence as if he has suddenly jumped into his clerical robes and our conversation is now to be 'pure' and 'holy.' Bill simply starts talking to God, and there we are, the three of us, communicating together. Bill never makes it them (the holy guys) against me (the bad guy)."

"I've always had a horrible suspicion that I was probably one of the 'bad' guys, and I've never liked the feeling. Say, Ginilou, was there ever a time in your life when you didn't pray?"

"Yes."

"*Yes?* That surprises me! Tell me about it."

"Well, there was a period in my life when, if things could possibly go bad, they continued right on past bad, three-quarters-and-a-half into worse. Everything was on a downhill slide and I couldn't find even a twig to grab. It seemed to me that every time I tried to pray, God was 'out to lunch.' I kept remembering a little sign that I had seen when I was a child at Emlenton Camp Meeting in Pennsylvania. The sign was in the back window of Reverend Nick Powell's car and it said, 'Everyone told me to cheer up—things could be worse. And so I cheered up and sure enough, things got worse!' At the time I thought it was very funny. But when I was in the middle of 'worse-getting-worser-going-straight-down-the-porcelain-facility,' I tell you, it wasn't funny anymore!

"I was pregnant, forty years old, in the middle of a divorce, and all alone. I mean, *alone!* My parents came for a short visit, and in the middle of the first night they were there, my dad got up in the dark and fell down the stairs and broke his arm. At that very moment my prayer went like this:

" 'Dad is hurt really bad and I'd surely like to talk to you about it, but it seems to me that recently when I come to you to talk things over, things have really gotten botched up. Right now I'm not at all sure I can handle any more trouble, so if my coming to you means that things are going to go from terrible to horrid—then please, oh, please just forget that I'm talking to you tonight. OK?'

"Then three nights later, as Mom and Dad were somewhere on the highway between where I was living and where they were living in Florida, I started up those same fatal steps to go to bed. Right then, without one sign of warning and four weeks early, my water broke.

"Need I tell you that the doctor couldn't be located? That the baby stopped moving? That I was sitting in the middle of my bed, alone, scared, in the dark. That this was the longest, loneliest night of my life?

"Now if you suppose that things improved

wonderfully when daylight arrived, you are wrong. The only thing that daylight improved was my ability to see without turning on the lights.

"Finally, midmorning, after examining me and taking X-rays, the doctor told me that he would have to perform a Caesarean section. I made the mistake of asking him what the baby's chances were. He said, 'Not good—not good at all. In fact, not any better than yours.'

"In a voice that I barely recognized as my own, I requested, 'Doctor, please don't put me to sleep. I want to be awake or I fear I'll never wake up.'

" 'That'll be up to the anesthetist,' he said crisply and left the room.

"They wheeled me to the delivery room door and left me alone while waiting for the anesthetist to arrive. Now ask me if I prayed."

"Did you pray?" Rob asked.

"Yes, I did. Are you ready for my prayer?"

"Yes, what was it?"

"*Help!*"

"That's it?"

"That's it!"

"And did he? Help, I mean."

"Well, Rob, you have to understand our relationship, God's and mine. We're really not very conventional. Sometimes we don't fit anyone's pattern except our own.

"You see, God didn't whomp up a little miracle and zap it off in my direction. The angels did not start singing. The nurses did not all radiate sweetness and light. The doctor's bad mood did not mellow. And all my relatives did not come

swinging down the corridor singing 'For She's a
Jolly Good Fellow.' "

"What *did* happen?"

"In the quiet, alone in that hallway, I found a
~~half-ounce~~ of courage that helped me grit my
teeth and just sorta hang in there. It seemed to
me God said, 'Hold on, Kid. You do your part, I'll
do mine. Just don't give up yet.' "

"And did they put you to sleep?"

"Nope, I watched it all. The anesthetist stroked
my forehead and talked to me in gentle tones.
And after what seemed to be an eternity, I heard
him say, in his Oriental accent, 'Doctors, best
finish quickly now. I cannot give her anything
else.'

"The doctors said, 'We need at least five more
minutes.'

" 'Sorry, Doctors, she has feeling now.'

" 'We'll hurry!'

"The anesthetist kept touching me and talking
to me and I concentrated on breathing—a lot!
Finally, one doctor said, 'Ginilou, you haven't
forgotten how to make a beautiful baby girl!' And
I watched in the mirror as he lifted Autumn
Dawn from her warm world inside of me.

"In measured tones the doctor said, 'Quickly,
they're both too weak! Give the baby to her
mother!' And so I talked to her.

"Oh, Baby Girl Mine—
　　your skin is as soft
　　as the petals of a gardenia,
　　your hair is black as soot.
　　You are so tiny,

so fragile . . .
Oh, Baby Girl Mine—
    I'll make you a deal,
    If you will try to keep on breathing
    so will I."

Rob sat quietly for a moment, then he spoke. "Ginilou, did God say anything then?"

"Seemed to me, he said, 'OK, you two. Hang in there!' And up to now, we have!"

"That's gutsy!"

"Gutsy?"

"Yeah. You don't like the word?"

"Umm . . . noooo . . . not particularly."

"OK, we'll find another one. You know, sometimes I've toyed around with the idea of using one or two words to describe people. I like trying to find a word that describes a person so well that another would immediately know what that person was like just by hearing that one word."

"And what word, Rob, do you feel describes you best?"

"I don't want you to laugh at me now, but I like two words for me. I like 'compassionate intellectual.' How do you like it?"

"Ummm, it'll do. But I'll tell you this much, I like your descriptive words a whole lot better for you than I like 'gutsy' for me!"

"OK, what word do you want to describe you?"

"I don't think I'd want to know what word really describes me best—and I doubt that I'd like the words that some people who *think* they know me would use to describe me, but if I had

a choice of the word that I *wish* described
me . . . I'd choose 'earthy' every time!
"I like it!

"Earthy is the smell of musk
    and rich, black earth lying in soft clumps.
Earthy is barefoot
    and tanned;
      daisies and violets.
Earthy is home-baked bread,
    a deep throaty laugh,
      steady eyes,
    and a strong handshake.
Earthy is more than sexy—
earthy is vibrant, alive, aware.
I choose 'earthy.' "

Aunt Nonie was earthy—she lived in Illinois.
Aunt Maggie was whiny and demanding;
Aunt Edith was stiff and rigid;
Aunt Rose was joy and laughter;
Aunt Ruby was perfect.
But Aunt Nonie was earthy—and I doubt that
anyone knew—except me—and, of course, the
men. The women never suspected.

She was not petite, or breathtakingly beautiful,
stylish, or soft-spoken—but, boy, she was earthy.
She smelled of freshly-tilled soil or strawberry
shortcake, sunshine or ham steak and gravy.
Whatever—she always smelled yummy! Her eyes
danced with sheer delight at what was unsaid
and unseen.

She laughed from her shoe soles upward to at
least four inches above the top of her head and

out from her body six inches in all directions. She knew how to laugh! And when the men looked at her, they saw a genuine woman.

Earthy!

I choose to be earthy.

"Don't think that I've ever heard a woman say that she wanted to be earthy. I've heard beautiful, brilliant, sexy. I've heard all that. But never have I heard 'earthy,'" Rob said, looking at me.

"Well, now you have. I choose earthy."

"Ginilou," Rob leaned close to me, wiggled his eyebrows, and said in a whisper, "You know, of course, that many people immediately hear 'earthy' only as 'good at making love.'"

"So?"

"They just might expect you to prove it."

"Why? If I say I'm good at baking a cake, do you expect me to rush to the closest kitchen and whip up a three-layer chocolate delight? If I tell you that I'm good at singing, do you expect that I'll stand there in the middle of the aisle and do three choruses of 'Suwannee'? If I tell you that I'm a good artist, do you believe that I'll zap out a sketch pad and instantly do your portrait? Well, do you?"

"Gee!" Rob said in a tone reminiscent of the late Jack Benny, "now that you've put it *that* way . . . no! But I think love is supposed to be different, isn't it?"

"Why? Why do we have to be so careful when speaking of love? I'm talking of love—not some casual relationship masquerading as love, but real love! If I ever get the chance, I'd like to speak out joyously, whimsically, and defensively of a positive love relationship, whether it is a man/woman relationship or God/man relationship. No big differences, no big distinction, just simple, uncomplicated, that-without-which-we-cannot-live love! Rob, earthy is not pornographic, dirty, or vulgar! Earthy is the musk of meaningful living, the salt in bread.

"To me, love and emotion are not sinful. Why can't we accept and acknowledge the good in the urges and feelings instilled within us long, long ago when God's quicksilver fingers scooped up a handful of mud and fashioned a man? Sometimes people act as if they thought it was perfectly holy and wonderful for God to watch while he made a man in his own image, but that he surely didn't—wouldn't have, mercy alive, *couldn't* have—peeked while he sculpted woman! They act as if he must have closed his eyes then!

"When, and if, I fall in love again, I'll want him to know that he may have prettier, sexier, smarter females interested in him, but he will never have anyone who thinks more about him—and who wants to pleasure him more than I.

"Oh, yes, I'm good at loving, baking a cake, writing a poem, singing a song, painting a "happy" . . . and I'm earthy!"

8:00 P.M.

"It's odd to me," Rob said, "that I'm talking to you the way I am. It seems stupid to say that I never confide in anyone when that is exactly what I've been doing!"

"Does that bother you?"

"Yes. Yes, it does."

"Why?"

"It bothers me to think that someone, a stranger at that, would really know me—be able to 'figure me out.' "

"Aha! If you let me know the real you then maybe I'll be able to figure out all the deep, dark, sinister, tricky things inside you. Then I'll be able to push some magic button and all of your mean, dirty thoughts will tumble out like marbles all over the floor for everyone to see!"

"You make it sound so silly, but, yes—something like that. And it does bother me!"

"Oh, Rob! Are your inner thoughts really so terrible?"

"Sometimes, if I'm being truthful with you, yes. Sometimes they are. Come on, Ginilou, 'fess up—aren't some of *your* thoughts sinister and dirty, too?"

"I confess that I don't share my inner thoughts with many people, and some thoughts I share with no one. But it's not because I think they are evil or dirty."

"Come to think about it, off-color thoughts don't go very well with your image, Ginilou!"

"Now you've brought up one of my biggest aggravations, and at the moment, I'm ignoring your 'off-color' reference. It upsets me that we decide what a person's 'image' is and then we won't allow him the right to be himself if it goes against our preconceived image.

"In the book I wrote I introduced many people. I wanted to portray them in great detail to be so accurate that should a reader run into them on the street, he'd recognize them immediately. The problem is this: I portrayed a part of the individual that was exposed in that particular incident and at that particular moment. After my manuscript had been read, some questions were put to me concerning 'Doc,' one of the main characters. And someone said, 'Oh, please don't tell me that about Doc, it doesn't fit at all with his image!'

"I felt like saying, 'I beg your pardon? Doesn't fit with his image? Who knew him best—you or I? Doc was more than a white-coated physician, he was a man! He played golf—badly, but he played! He spoke eight languages (and English was definitely not his most fluent). He yelled a lot, he hated cats, he ate cold boiled potatoes for breakfast on Sunday morning, he put garlic on almost everything, he loved Alvin and the Chipmunks, he sang off-key, he liked mustard on anything that wasn't nailed down 'cept breakfast cereal. What do you mean "doesn't fit with his image"? It was Doc!'

"Why can't we let people be themselves? Some people who have never met me have read my book and decided what type of person I am. They think I'm a person who always reaches out in love, that I am always *aware,* and that God's love spills off my fingertips like water dripping from a leaky faucet—that my inner thoughts are, by their definition, 'pure.'

"Truth is, most often I stumble into the wrong place at the wrong time. I speak when I should have listened, I listen when I should have spoken. Occasionally my mind, my mouth, my eyes, and my ears work together! And that's good! But the rest—getting mad, sulking in a corner, pushing the 'pull' door, and trying to go up the 'down' escalator—that's me too!

"And my thoughts? They are mine and let me tell you that they *are* pure, by my definition. They often are filled with love—

love for people,
God's love,
family love,
romantic love—
and, I tell you, it is purely good!
And that's me, too, as I feel God intended!"

61

"Ah, Ginilou, are you telling me that my 'sexy' thoughts aren't dirty?" Rob asked me with a gleam in his eyes.

"No, I'm not! I'm only telling you that *mine* aren't!"

"Ginilou, you mentioned that you worked for a doctor. Did you like the work?"

"Sometimes."

"Did you like him?"

"Sometimes."

"I'm afraid that some of my employees only like me 'sometimes' too! I'd ask if you had a good working relationship with the good doctor, but you'd just say 'sometimes.' "

"No, I wouldn't. We always had a good working relationship. We didn't always agree and there were times when I drove him to his wits' end and almost plumb up the wall. But we always worked well together. I had tremendous respect for his abilities, and he had an appreciation for whatever it was he had me there for!"

"What *did* you do there?"

"A dab of everything."

"What I mean is, what did he pay you for?"

"Mostly, he paid me for my intuition."

"There must have been more to it than that! I can't quite imagine a medical office run on intuition."

"I didn't say that I 'ran' the office—the office was well-staffed and well-'run.' But most of the happenings that took place in the office where I spent my time ran on intuition.

"People do not always fit into readily definable categories. Sometimes, a great deal depends on finding something that isn't quite in evidence as yet."

"I don't think that I would function well in the life-and-death types of situations that exist in a doctor's office. I find that I pull away from even simple pain and illness. I'm not exactly sure why, Ginilou, but I find myself very uncomfortable and uneasy whenever I have to face illness."

"Wish I could say that you are in a minority or that there is an easy cure for your malady, but I can't. It seems that many people have the very same difficulty.

"When I heard that my friend Woody had had a stroke, I dropped what I was doing and rushed to the hospital. Woody was lying in bed, eyes closed, pale—not a visible movement of any sort. He looked much like a sleeping, scared little boy. Jaye, his wife, was sitting in a chair at the foot of the bed, and she appeared to be so calm that I felt my fear subsiding.

"Jaye is one of the world's special people. An original, no carbon copy. She is chock-full of the spirit of God. If ever a godly woman lived, it is Jaye. She is no plastic saint, has no 'holier than thou' attitude or ashes and sackcloth spirit. She's just a good, solid, barefoot, down-to-earth, godly woman!

"Later, much later, Jaye brought Woody home, against advice. Medical opinion was that Woody would never again walk, or talk, or be Woody. But that opinion was given minus the knowledge of Woody's determination, Jaye's support, their combined faith and love, and God's power.

"Time passed, as time does, sometimes slowly,

sometimes swiftly. Today, Woody walks, 'n talks, 'n Woody *is*. However, one of the regrettable things between his stroke and functioning anew was that many people stayed away from Jaye and Woody because they didn't know how to act and what to say!

"And some who did visit angered me to tears. They reminded me of some of the people who had visited my beloved Granddaddy after he had his stroke. People who I had always assumed had some degree of intelligence would speak of Granddaddy (as they now did of Woody) as if he were not in the room. If they acknowledged him at all, they would scream in his face as if he were deaf, and speak in a ridiculous type of baby-talk as if he were retarded!

"In both cases, after witnessing such stupid antics, I'd fight the ever-increasing anger within me and clench my teeth to keep from screaming. I'd walk out of the room, out of the house, and go fishing. It made no sense to others, but it made sense to me. Both men were avid fisher-men, so I'd go fishing on the lake to grow calm. Then I had something to go back and talk to them about."

"I wish I could get rid of my uneasiness with illness," Rob said. "I'm sure I'd be no good at all in the face of death! Tell me, how could you bear looking at people and knowing that they wouldn't make it? I think I would heartily avoid encoun-ters like that."

"Rob, I didn't figure you for one of those people who read the last page of a book first!"

"I'm not! But what has that to do with this?"

"Well, some people treat their relationships the same way. They want to see the ending before they make the decision as to whether or not they want to invest their time and energy in reading the whole book.

"Once upon a time there was a little boy called 'Shuggie.' . . . I wrote about him in *It's About Love*. Shuggie's own mother pulled away from this beautiful child because she was incapable of facing the fact that he was dying. She had looked at the end and from that moment on, in her heart, he was already gone.

"Whatever the relationship—sickness or health—I don't feel it is fair to start at the end. It is too limiting. I figure we just have to take today and give what we have to give to each other now. I don't believe we ought to write the ending before the first line is finished."

There was simply no way that Joe could make it. None. His was not a happy diagnosis: multiple sclerosis.

Happy, carefree Joe. Joe, who sprinted through life the same way he took a football field— surefootedly, determined, proud.

Within the walls of my office Joe was always in command—forever the coach—and I cheered him on as he filled cassette tape after cassette tape with his unique legacy of stories and poems for his family.

It wasn't easy to face Joe's dying. It wasn't easy to face Joe's death. But it couldn't be avoided.

Then one day there was a rap at my door.

"Ginilou?"

"Yes?"

"May I come in?"

"Certainly." I pushed aside the papers I was working on. "Have a seat."

She was a tall, well-dressed woman. She moved so gracefully that I could easily picture her dancing in a ballet or running, in slow motion, through a pile of leaves in the fall. There was something magnetic about her. She sat across from me and looked at me directly, unblinking. She had the largest, saddest brown eyes I had ever encountered.

"Is there something I can do for you?" I inquired.

"I am Kate. Kate Morrison. Joe spoke of you so often. You gave him back a reason to live as long as he could, and a way to die with dignity." Her eyes filled with unshed tears and her voice broke.

"Kate," I said, "I'm so pleased to meet you. Joe loved you so much. It was a joy to hear the pride and love in his voice whenever he spoke of you. I'm glad you're here. How are you?"

"How am I? Oh, I hate to be asked that question. How am I? I don't know. I hurt inside—sometimes so much I could die. And then sometimes I feel nothing. There are other times I am so angry that I scare myself!"

"I'm sure it isn't easy. How are the boys?"

"I don't know that either. They smile so much when they're around me. No one could feel that good. No one could really want to smile as much as they smile at me."

"It's only because they care, Kate. Tell me, how can I help?"

She shook her head as if to clear it and, after a long pause, she said, "Ginilou, I've come to see you because Joe loved you so deeply. And because he said that you would have something for me when I needed it." Her voice broke. "I need it now."

"Joe told you that I had something to give you?"

"Yes."

"Did he tell you what it was?"

"No. He only said that, if I needed to, I should come to see you and that you would have something to give me. And so I've come today."

"Why today instead of tomorrow, or yesterday, or last week, or next month? Why today?"

"Because today is the day I can't get through." She looked away from me and I could see the muscles tighten in her face as she struggled for composure and won.

I picked up the telephone and buzzed the secretary. "Cancel my afternoon appointments. I'll be out of the office until closing time."

Then I buzzed Doc. "Kate Morrison is here. I'll be out of the office with her until 5:30 or so."

"I'll be right in," Doc said. "I've meant to call Kate. I want to ask her how she is."

"No, not yet." And I hung up before he could protest.

I motioned for Kate to follow me and we went out and got into my car and I started driving.

"Where are we going, Ginilou?"

"I don't know, Kate . . . we're just getting through today."

Neither of us said anything. It was not a time for chitchat—or deep soul-searching.

I pulled into the zoo parking lot and we walked through the iron gates. In some ways, it was as if we had suddenly stepped into another world. The stillness that had engulfed us in the closed, air-conditioned car was gone. Sunshine embraced everything, and there were the brightly-colored faces of flowers dancing in the summer breeze and the bright, laughing faces of children scampering along the pathways.

We walked till we were tired and then settled ourselves on a bench to watch the antics of the monkeys. I heard Kate chuckle and she pointed to an especially comical little fellow hiding a banana from his companion.

The minutes ticked away in the afternoon sun and we laughed and talked—or sat in silence— as we pleased.

Then Kate began to speak of Joe, and it was good.

"Ginilou," she said at long last, "I am so full of grief, but right now I feel stirrings inside of me that I can't explain. Strange stirrings not unlike those I felt years ago when I first learned I was pregnant. I wonder what it all means."

"You mean 'stirrings' as in feelings you can't describe—like 'yearning' or 'craving'?" I asked.

"Yes, like that."

"Oh, Kate, you have a craving for life, a yearning to live! You've fought to keep memories of Joe all buried away because you didn't want to hurt anymore. But it isn't Joe's memories that hurt you, it's his death! It's OK to be sad that Joe died. But don't grieve over his memory. Memories of Joe are pleasant and happy—enjoy them! Don't bury yourself and his memories with him!

"You know, I have a friend who likes popcorn. He has a passion for hot buttered popcorn. He more than likes it—he loves it, he craves it! And it so happens that ever since I was knee-high to a turkey-bird I've made the best popcorn in the whole wide world! Sometimes I make hot buttered popcorn. Sometimes I melt caramels and make hot caramel corn. Sometimes I throw in a handful of nuts with the caramels and make, well, I don't know what—but it's *yumm!* Now as long as my friend stays at his house, lying on the couch daydreaming and craving popcorn—he doesn't have any! No matter how much he wishes he had some, he hasn't got nary a mouthful!

"Kate, you're craving life, but no matter how much you yearn to live—if you stay at home, burying memories of Joe, you haven't got any!"

"You're right," she said slowly. "Ginilou, tonight would you come over to our house? I'll stop on the way home and pick up some popcorn and caramels and nuts and you come over and show me how to make that concoction of yours. Tomorrow I'll take some over to the crippled children's hospital where I used to do volunteer work. I might even bring a couple of kids out here to the zoo."

And the afternoon was gone and it was time to leave.

Back at the office, when our laughter had died

away after one of Kate's favorite stories about Joe's football days, she said, "Ginilou, Joe didn't leave you anything for me, did he?"

"No, Kate. He didn't."

Kate laughed a warm, low, throaty laugh, "That Joe! He knew I wouldn't come to see you unless I had a reason for coming. But he knew I'd need someone to talk to, someone to help me 'sort it out' . . . someone to care. Ginilou, the package Joe sent me for was you."

Kate got in her car and I watched her drive away.

The months and years have come and gone and still occasionally, while watching some football game on television, I'll see a player run onto the field with a certain style that reminds me of Joe. And always I remember the words Kate said to me before she drove away.

"It's important to know that in the presence and loss of great love, life must go on—or else the value of that love is lost forever!"

8:10 P.M.

"Ginilou, you're staring at that lady in the blue suit. Do you know her?"

"No."

"What do you find so interesting about her?"

"A while ago you told me that you would like to believe that we're here to help one another instead of stepping on one another."

"So?"

"So, here's your chance to prove it. Now it is altogether possible that anyone on this airplane could say the words that will help that woman, but most likely none of them will. So, you have an excellent opportunity to 'pay up' for being a member of the human race. You can help."

"How?"

"Well, look at her, Rob. What do you see?"

"I guess she's attractive—certainly no raving beauty, but she borders on being attractive. I see nothing about her that indicates that she needs help of any kind."

"Just watch her for a minute! She keeps checking her watch, so I'd guess she is getting off at our next stop. I'd also say she's on her way to see someone important to her. She smoothes her skirt, adjusts her necklace, sighs deeply. But now watch—she's going to frown and look down at her shoes. Then she'll tap her teeth with a fingernail and look over quizzically at that shoe case under the seat in front of her."

"My gosh, she is! How did you know that?"

"She's done the same thing several times. She seems really pleased with her hair, her outfit, her nails, everything but those shoes. She just isn't sure about those shoes being right, and she's really wondering about changing them."

"I don't see anything wrong with her shoes."

"Me neither. In fact, they're very attractive."

"So, what is it that you suggest I do?"

"Go over there and, in your own style, compliment her shoes. Then watch what happens."

"You're going to get my face slapped for me! That's what will happen!"

"Chicken!"

"Oh boy, that did it!"

"I thought perhaps it might."

"Ginilou, you sure are weird!"

"Bye, Rob, have fun!"

"I'm going, I'm going!"

If you didn't rent shoe skates, it didn't cost very much to go skating.

The skating rink was a different world from the one I was used to. The music was bright and loud and bouncy. It made me want to move and laugh. Beautiful girls wore short, swirly skirts and elegant skates that laced up their legs.

I didn't go skating very often. Being a P.K. (Preacher's Kid) there just wasn't much extra money. But occasionally, on a Saturday afternoon when the kids from the Methodist church were going to the rink, I was invited to go along. We'd all meet at their church parsonage and the minister would say, "Hello, sweetheart, and how is your father?"

I would say, "Just fine, sir."

Then he would always explain to someone that I was the daughter of his minister friend who pastored the church up the street.

I would try to stand still, look politely interested in what he was saying (as if it were the first time I'd heard it). He'd pat my shoulder and beam, "We like doing things together." I'd smile and wish it were time to leave.

When we'd get to the rink I'd put my skates on and go off by myself to practice over at the side of the floor. Mostly I'd just try not to fall down. I was too frightened to go out on the floor where all the skaters were laughing and having so much fun.

I'd watch the pretty, older girls gracefully gliding by. Some of them could even skate backwards. I wished I could do that, but I could barely stand up frontwards.

Then—always—my skates would come unfastened at the toe and clatter and bang as I hobbled over to a chair and tried to fix them tighter.

One Saturday, the minister's son was home

from college. Never, ever have I seen such a fuss made over any one individual! I watched while the girls smiled and turned, giggled and looked all sparkly-eyed. *They seem silly and excited, like a bunch of hens around the new rooster,* I thought to myself as my skates once again came unfastened and I hobbled to the side.

"No wonder you're having trouble there," a voice said. "Those things don't fit you." I looked up to find the minister's son smiling at me.

He took away the clangy, clamp-on skates and brought back a beautiful pair of white shoe skates. He put them on my feet and helped me to stand. And then—oh!

I can't believe it!

Great Leapin' Lizards!

While the grown-up girls watched jealously, he guided me from the sidelines out onto the polished floor!

He didn't leave me for the rest of the afternoon. Whenever a pouty voice said, "You haven't skated with me all afternoon," he would just smile and say, "How can I possibly leave just now? We P.K.'s have a great deal to talk about, you know."

He'd wink at me like we had a big secret and I'd feel my face getting warmer and warmer. I'd look down at those beautiful skates and smile— and wish my ankles didn't hurt so much!

He tipped my chin so I had to look at him, and he said, "Remember now, that's a beautiful smile. Don't give it to the skates. Let me see it! Let the world see it! There. That's better. Hey, you're doing fine. You're really going to be a good skater. You know, with that smile and those eyes you're really going to be a heartbreaker when you grow up!"

I don't remember exactly all we talked about. But I *do* remember the feel of his strong hands holding me up. I remember the long smooth strides I tried to match, his smile, the warmth of my face, laughter shared, my sweaty hands, and the confidence I gained to skate. And something more important he taught me—about taking the time to be observant and responsive, about being sensitive and giving compliments, and about being daring enough to leave the sidelines and step out confidently into the mirrored spotlight of life.

I've forgotten his last name. His first name? Perhaps it was Joe. Now that I think of it, yes, it was Joe. But the kindness and the warmth are unforgettable. And they come to me again and again when I need them most.

8:15 P.M.

Rob eased back into the seat beside me.

"Well? Tell me about it."

"I did what you said. I've never felt so nervous over such a little thing! But she smiled at me and thanked me and she didn't poke me in my nose."

Rob leaned back in his chair and closed his eyes. "However, I *still* don't see that I helped anything at all."

"OK, Smarty, open your eyes now and look at what you've accomplished." He looked at the woman and his eyes widened. There she sat— c-a-l-m—her arms at rest, a slight smile on her face, a confident look in her eyes—completely ready!

"And I did that?"

"Looks like it!"

"Well, what do you know! When she isn't frowning, she really is very pretty."

"You noticed, huh?"

"I noticed! Ginilou, a bit ago you said something about my having a chance to 'pay up' for being a member of the human race. I rather like that idea."

"Most often we never really know when we're 'paying up,' when something we do turns out to be the hand up that someone desperately needed."

"Well, you've given *me* a 'hand up,' as you say, just by being so candid with me. Any particular person responsible for providing you with a hand up?"

"Oh, more than one. But I'll tell you of one in particular. A couple of years ago I was about six steps below the level where well-meaning people lean out and yell down at you, 'Listen, sister, other people are worse off than you are! What you have to do is just concentrate and pull yourself up by your own bootstraps!' Well, honestly, I am not totally stupid, contrary to some people's evaluation. If I could have pulled myself up, I certainly would have done so! The fact is, not only didn't I know where my bootstraps were, I wasn't even sure which direction was 'up'!

"About that time, Tim Kufeldt, my daughter Stormi's 'best-est' buddy who is accepted as part of the family and who knows the inside of my refrigerator better than I do, came over to visit. He brought me a little book to read. He was enthusiastic about it and anxious for me to read it. After he left, I halfheartedly began reading.

"I started at the beginning. I read every page, top to bottom, left to right. I turned the page, and repeated the process. I read and read, and was bored to oblivion until the third line down in a poem on page sixty-eight. There in bold type were the words, **except you.**

"I flipped back one page and reread:

I was thinking about God.
He sure has plenty of children—
plenty of artists,
plenty of singers,
and carpenters,
and candlestick makers,
and preachers,
plenty of everybody . . .
except you
and all of them together
can never take your place.

"Well, *now* I was awake and aware! I immediately stopped reading and turned back to the title, *Come Share the Being* by Bob Benson. I began reading again. I started at the beginning. I read each page, top to bottom, left to right, turned the page, and repeated the process. I read and read, and was thrilled beyond belief!

"I laughed and chortled. I 'felt,' I agreed. I identified. Now I found all the prime nuances. I couldn't believe it was the same book!

"Since then I've read and reread that book. The print is almost worn off the pages. It was my 'hand up.'

"The point is, Bob Benson didn't write that book just for me! He had no idea there was a 'ginilou' who needed those words. He had no idea that certain people had been trying to force me into their 'acceptable pigeonhole' and make me into someone I wasn't—something other than me—all in the name of religion. He wrote a book for people. I read words for me. It was his way of 'paying up' for being a member of the family of man. It was my 'hand up.' "

"Where can I get that book?" Rob asked.

"From my purse. I'll let you have my copy. I have another at home."

"So what you're saying is that 'paying up' can happen even when you aren't aware that you're doing it."

"Sometimes, yes. Sometimes.

"One Sunday evening I went to church early so I could practice the organ a bit. Later, I eased off the organ bench and sat down on a pew behind the organ where I could see but not be seen.

"In the gathering evening dusk several women shuffled through the sanctuary doors, down the aisle, and arranged themselves on one of the pews about halfway on the right side of the church.

"They didn't speak much. Their faces were drawn and tired. Their shoulders were pitched forward, eyes downcast. Silence loomed and the darkness deepened, punctuated now and then by a quivering sigh.

"Then the doors flew open and down the aisle burst Jim, a tall, broad-shouldered, handsome man singing loudly in his rich baritone.

"Walking beside him was Jean, a pretty, petite woman in a white pantsuit, laughingly shushing him.

"And, as I watched, a miracle happened! Jean paused for a moment, leaned down, and pressed her cheek against Bessie's wrinkled forehead—and Bessie's eyes 'turned on.'

"Jean touched another woman on the arm and smiled into another's face. One by one she touched each woman with her magic wand of self.

"Jim held out his hand, firmly grasped each lady's hand in his, gazed deeply into her eyes, and grinned a crinkly grin that I'm sure could be felt from her wrinkled face clear down to her sturdy heeled shoe.

"*Shazam!* The 'little ole ladies' disappeared and in their places sat vital, glowing women!

"For an instant, they were reminded by a young woman how it feels to be alive. For an instant, they were reminded by a vibrant man how it feels to be a woman. Jim and Jean weren't even aware that by giving of themselves, they were paying up their membership dues in the family of man.

"Even if I'm unaware?" asked Rob. "Even if it is in my line of work, I can still be paying up! Right?"

"Uhhh, well . . . only if it is done sincerely and not for the purpose of standing around after-wards, taking a bow, and waiting for the angels to start singing a rousing heavenly chorus of 'Thou Art Truly a Magnificent Human Being Worthy of All Praise, Saint Rob.' "

"Got it! But now, Ginilou, explain something to me, if you can. Let's say that I am *willing* to pay up—I honestly want to be of help. You know, some people are so effective at hiding their needs you can't tell if they're teetering on the edge. What is it that lets you know?"

"I can try to answer that, but I'm not sure I can explain just exactly what it is."

"Something must have taught you to recognize pain. What was it?"

"Not a something, Rob, a some*one!* Someone who had to deal with many kinds of pain.

"And over the years I've learned that whether it's actual physical pain or throbbing psychological spasms—whether it's shown by

a flicker in the eyes,
a fluttering movement of the hands,
a turning of the face to the wall,
a piercing scream in the night from
    a sixteenth-floor window ledge—
pain, real pain,
all looks the same!"

It was a long way from Pennsylvania to Kentucky. But once a year without fail, Mother, Dad, and I made the trip to visit the family.

Lying back in the backseat of the car with the smell of the scratchy upholstery filling my head and making me sick to my tummy, I'd close my eyes and think about the pretty lady we would see first—Aunt Georgia.

Aunt Georgia would gather me in her soft arms and smooth my hair and kiss my face and lead me into the house. She'd have a glass of cold lemonade waiting for me when I came out of the bathroom, and then we'd go into the living room to "rest." The adults would do the catch-up talk that would bring everything into focus after a year of being apart, while I was soothed into a half-sleep lying on Aunt Georgia's flowered couch. Her cool fingers caressed my ears and her light, flowery perfume replaced the sickening odor of hot days of travel. Her laughter sounded like the tinkling of a jeweled wind chime, and if her speech had been any more Southern, you couldn't have understood her at all! It was all marvelously delightful!

But it was her eyes that fascinated me most. They could be bright and flashing with rainbows of inaudible laughter, or deepening with empathy, or filled with the questions of a most inquisitive mind. Still, at all times, behind them—there at the deepest point—was a thin veil of sadness that never entirely disappeared.

There were gatherings at the park where Uncle Sam swung me high into the air on an old swing with its rusty, squeaky chain and its broad-board seat. Aunt Georgia's laugh floated to us on the edge of a breeze filled with the inviting smells of frying hamburgers and crackling hot dogs. There was laughter, kisses tasting of mustard, all the food we could eat, the sounds of fun, and the slap that followed the mosquito's bite. Through it all the veil remained securely in place behind Aunt Georgia's friendly, loving eyes.

Later, when I had learned to accept the strange paradoxical look and no longer questioned its existence, I learned that her first love and their children had died tragically. In my child's mind I figured out that the veil was where the pain had gone to hide.

When Sammy was born to Aunt Georgia and Uncle Sam our visits had an added dimension. Now there was a boy's room filled to the walls with a roaring, whistling, chugging train.

Between visits pictures were passed back and forth across the states, courtesy the United States mail. At first there was a laughing baby child lying on his tummy on the living room rug. Later there was an impish boy standing beside a pony and squinting into the camera's lens. And not long after, we received a picture of a gangling, uncoordinated young'un hanging upside down from a backyard tree.

Then, one day, the phone rang. The telephone in our living room gave no warning that, of all the messages it had brought to us in the past, this one now demanding to be heard would be among those we least wanted to receive.

A car had careened across the main street of town up over the curb, pinning Aunt Georgia, who had been window-shopping, in the wreckage of a department store window. With a crushed pelvis, two broken legs, a concussion, and minus her left arm, she hovered between Now and Never.

Months later I walked into her bedroom at home where they had brought her to rest between operations. She was encased, like a mummy, from her chin to her toes. And when I saw her, I was grateful she was asleep.

I knew that she must be in unimaginable

physical pain, and I couldn't help wondering just what I'd see when the real Aunt Georgia opened her eyes and looked out at me from all the bandages and plaster.

Actually, I thought, it could be *anybody* lying there—but it wasn't. She opened her eyes, eyes now bright with fever, but it was Aunt Georgia— still with that same thin veil of sadness . . . or was it pain?

And, since that time, whenever, wherever I see that look (or one like it), I recognize real pain. Sometimes it is physical hurt, sometimes it is mental anguish—but always it is pain.

"Ginilou, surely there are degrees of pain. A sprained ankle is not the same as an amputated leg!"

"I beg your pardon! I never said that! You wanted to know what teaches someone to recognize pain. I assumed you meant when there is no immediately visible evidence that there is pain. But what I'm saying is any pain is real!

"George Davidson, who has contributed more to my philosophy of life than anyone outside my parents, is in *real pain*. He has been since the year one, it seems. Years ago his left leg had to be amputated. Since then George has had to live each moment as a permanent partner with pain. Somehow he learned to function in spite of it all. Still I am sure there are times when it is so unbearable that if he could have pressed a button that would have ended it all without causing his beloved wife, Ruth, and his daughter,

Becky, any pain, he would have *pressed* it with real relief—and a smile of gratitude. George is no weakling—no sit-on-the-sidelines complainer. I'm simply telling you that his pain is that excruciating.

"I am told that phantom pain is experienced by all amputees. They say at times it is almost unendurable! In some cases, divorce, death, and separation produces the same rigorous phantom pain. In *both* instances, the brain and the body scream out for help and lunge for any straw of acceptable relief.

"One afternoon I received a phone call from a friend: 'Go take care of Betty. I can't. Do what you can for her, please.' So I went to Betty. I didn't know her well, but I went to her. For the next few months, we were closer than most people ever become. What is important is that she was in pain—real pain. Rejected, denied, deserted—abandoned not only by her husband, but by her church and by those she had considered her closest friends. She was in the midst of emotional amputation and real pain! At that time, George and Betty shared a common look. A look that communicated their experience of pain—torturous and real. A pain that can't be erased by a pat on the arm or a little pink pill."

8:30 P.M.

"Ginilou, you said that you believe in love. Do you also believe that there is such a thing as being in love with love?"

"Yes."

"When you're not really in love at all?"

"Yes, sometimes it happens that way."

"That's the way it was with us. Beth was pretty, and it was spring, and I must admit that physically she really knew how to get to me. Everyone seemed to think we'd get married, and the whole idea was exciting. Even flattering. I mean, she wanted *me*. And I wanted something permanent—or maybe I wanted some*one* permanent. And so . . ."

Rob's voice sounded like he was in great pain, and he rubbed his hands through his hair before he started speaking hesitantly again. "And so we got married. For a while it was nice, but it wasn't quite real."

"Playing house."

"What?"

"Playing house."

"Yes, exactly. Playing house. And soon, all too soon, that was all it was. We'd play 'happy husband and cutesy-poo wife' when we'd visit with our friends. But at home we just sort of slipped into a stalemate routine of sorts. Sometimes we'd fight. Mostly we just ignored each other."

"Did you fight just to make up?"

"Sometimes."

"Regrettable."

"She kept the house so clean I felt like I was living in a hotel. Sometimes I was sure that I was the only thing there that wasn't completely sterilized, sprayed with antiseptic, and encased in plastic."

"There were times when I envy women who delight in keeping their houses so clean," I said, smiling slightly.

"Don't!" Rob said emphatically. "When it's more important that the floor not be tracked up than it is to know that your husband has arrived home safely after a long day's work, then something is terribly out of balance."

"Maybe she wanted or needed something else to do."

"She did do something else. She kept her job when we got married. She wanted it that way. And that was fine.

"But then one day, I don't remember when, I realized I simply wasn't happy. I was lying on the couch half-listening to a game on television and half-daydreaming, and I couldn't remember exactly how many years I'd been lying there while she had been yelling at me over God only knows how many stupid, ridiculous things.

"There I was, an attorney—not exactly a total dummy—and she was always running me down about something or other, really going out of her way to hurt my feelings. All I was doing was existing. The happiest hours of my day were those that I spent at work. It's true. Sad, but true."

"What happened after all this realization set in?"

"I just gave up. I spent more and more time working—at the office, at home, anywhere. I kept busy at *anything*. When I was at home, I daydreamed. Are you a daydreamer, Ginilou?"

"Hey, are you kiddin'? Listen, as daydreamers go I happen to be a professional! For me, it's a sweet necessity, a filmy, cotton candy without which life's circus does not deserve to exist!"

In our daydreams . . .
> We have lain on the rug,
> watching the flames in the fireplace.
> We have watched the wind play hide-and-
> > seek
> in the tops of the pines on the mountain-
> > side.
We have talked of
> buttercups and war,
> hot buttered popcorn and wishes.
We have fished in
> mountain streams for speckled trout,
> and calm inland lakes for bass.

We have sailed
  the seas—
  and each other's emotions.
We have waded in slate-bottomed creeks together . . .
  and as the thunder rolled
  across the skies,
  I have hidden my face
  beneath your left ear,
  and you have laughed
  and raised my face to yours.
We have run through clover fields,
  trudged through fresh-fallen snow.
We have seen the wonder of
  what might have been
  in each other's eyes.
We have shared a thousand sighs
  and more . . .
  in our daydreams.

8:40 P.M.

"I'm sure that she had no idea how—," Rob began.

"She, who?" I broke in.

"She, Beth. I'm sure that Beth had no idea how I started to dread our time together. I couldn't talk it over with her. She was totally unapproach-able—hard, harsh. So I'd just go home and attend to whatever had to be done, exchange a few polite (or not so polite) words, then lie on the couch, read a book or watch television—and daydream. I don't know that she ever knew how much I grew to hate her disrupting my thoughts, intruding on my 'playtime.'

"When we made love, let's face it, after all those years, we knew how to make love. Mostly it was predictable, a set pattern, no variance. I would lie there in the dark feeling guilty because I didn't really love her, and because I had been thinking of some 'make-believe' lady.

"I haven't ever tried to put all of this into words, so it may not be very clear. It certainly isn't easy to explain, but mostly I was so convinced that somewhere there was a world, a place, where I would fit and belong so completely that whenever she interrupted my search for it, I felt almost uncontrollable anger.

"I began to feel the way I did as a boy when I'd lie outside under the trees and dream of a world where Joey and I had our mother back. She'd be terribly beautiful and would tell us that on that day so long ago a group of horrid men had kidnapped her because she was really the Queen of Somewhere. But now she had escaped and we'd all go away and live happily forevermore— Joey, Daddy, Mother, and me!

"I'd build such a wonderful world, and I simply cannot explain the all-consuming joy I would experience there. Then someone—usually some adult—would step right in the middle of my dream and dash it to bits and tear me to shreds. I began to hate them all—all the dream-smashers!"

Bobby could scarcely contain his excitement as he tugged and pulled me along to the Jacksons' garage.

"Wait'll ya see!" he shouted. "Jus' wait'll ya see! Boy, are we gonna have fun!"

Susie Jackson was jumping up and down beside the garage door and hollering, "Hurry up! Hurry up!"

Then we stepped inside.

Shazam!

The hard dirt floor was piled high with mounds of pale tan sand. None of us had ever seen so much sand all in one place before. For the next few days all of our play time was spent in the Jackson's garage.

Susie's father worked for Nabisco, and she brought in various sizes of white tin boxes that said "Nabisco Crackers" in red letters across the corner.

Bobby brought some old toy cars, part of a discarded train set, a couple of spools, a few tongue depressors, and buttons of various sizes.

Jeff's dad sold tires so he helped Bobby and Jeff roll a couple of old tires over to use in our play world.

Mother gave me spools of varying sizes, an empty perfume bottle, and a broken mirror from a blue enameled compact (that still smelled of pressed powder) to make a lake for the king's garden.

From somewhere we gathered bits and pieces of this and that and zillions of bottle caps to make our roads.

We each had our own special corner of sand to work in but no one ever drew lines or said, "This is mine—get out!"

Jeffrey asked me to make him a garden like mine, with benches around his castle, and I asked him to design my winding streets and a park.

Bobby found an old flashlight somewhere and he took all the "innards" out. He stood the case upright, fastened copper wire strands inside of it, and let them cascade out the top. The illusion it created was almost like a fountain. Right in the center of our world he placed the largest tin cracker canister and carefully sat the flashlight fountain in its middle. He placed small pebbles around the base to make it secure, filled the canister with water, and on the water floated two tiny sailboats and a rubber swan. It was gorgeous!

We didn't know what it was, but it was gorgeous! We didn't have anything to call his gorgeous creation, so it became the "bobby-made."

"I'm going over to the bobby-made and sail a boat."

"If you lie on your back and look up at the bobby-made, it looks like those big firecrackers that exploded at the park last summer."

One afternoon Bobby was a bit tired of building and he said, "Ginilou, can I come over to your castle and lie down?"

"OK."

But he accidentally pushed over the right wing of my castle. The rest of the afternoon he helped me build it back and, no doubt about it, it was much better than it had been before. Besides, it surely was a lot more fun building together!

From then on, I helped him build his beautiful bobby-mades, and then we'd rest outside my castle.

We transformed all that beautiful sand and our prized collectibles into the most elaborate, elegant world of sand castles and bobby-mades that we were capable of producing.

And it was our world,
set apart—
no noise,
no intrusion

no disharmony—
just perfection!

The weekend arrived and Bobby's and Susie's families went camping. Jeffrey visited his grandmother in Pittsburgh, and I stayed at home and went to Sunday school and church.

While the choir sang and Daddy preached, I figured out how to make a bed for my doll Janey out of a matchbox.

Monday morning Bobby yelled for me and we ran as fast as we could over to the Jacksons' garage. I carried Janey and Bobby carried the matchbox.

He opened the door and the sunlight streamed in and filtered through the broken window onto the smooth, clean, new cement floor!

In the corner by the door was an old box full of spools 'n bottles,
cars 'n trains,
bottle caps 'n buttons,
a broken mirror 'n an old flashlight.
Two old tires leaned against the wall.

I clutched Janey to me so she wouldn't be able to see all the horrible destruction.

Bobby twisted his right sneaker on the floor till it squeaked . . . he rubbed his left arm across his forehead . . .

"They shouldn't a' done it," he said. "They shouldn't a' done it. I hate them all."

A horn honked
and someone yelled
for someone else
who didn't answer.

"I hate them all."

94

8:45 P.M.

"I know you'll probably just tell me that I'm just being paranoid, but I honestly believe that there isn't one woman who wouldn't walk out on me."

"That figures."

"Why do you say that?"

"Because I'm sure that's the way you feel."

"Now look here," Rob began angrily and defensively, "I did *everything* to keep my wife. I didn't leave her—she left me. I wasn't happy, but I never tried to get her to leave. In fact, I did everything to keep her."

"I'm sure you did."

"Now what's *that* supposed to mean?"

"It means you don't have to be defensive with me. I believe you. It means I am sure you did what you could to see to it that she stayed."

"But I did. I really did!"

"That's what I said."

"I came home from a meeting one night and

she was gone. She had just packed up her things and moved out, leaving only a telephone number where she could be reached.

"I spent the whole night carefully looking at every side of the situation and trying to figure out just what I should say when I called her. It was a very long night, I tell you."

"And in the end, you didn't call her at all."

"No. I didn't call. As long as she was in our home I did everything to keep her there, but . . ." and he just sighed, shook his head, and waved his hand as if to dismiss the rest.

"But," I said, "when she was gone you did nothing to bring her back."

"It's better this way. Much better."

"I'm sure."

"Really! You can believe me! She is happy now, and I am . . . well, at least I'm no longer *un*happy. I think I'd really like to ask you how you know that I did nothing to bring her back. But I have this terrible sinking feeling that your reason would anger me."

"Perhaps."

"It *would* anger me, wouldn't it?"

"Oh, Rob, in all probability I could come up with a reason you wouldn't particularly like."

"Go ahead, Smarty!"

"Do you enjoy getting angry?"

"No, but I will enjoy telling you that you're wrong!"

"I see."

"So, tell me, after doing *everything* I could to keep her there, just why did I do nothing to get her back?"

"Just maybe you felt powerless to do anything else—in either situation. Either to end a hum-drum marriage, or to bring her back."

"Don't be stupid! That's just plain dumb! I'm a grown man. I could have done anything I wanted to."

"Ah, that is true. I know it, but I seriously doubt that *you* knew it."

"Explain!"

"You couldn't do anything to bring your mother back either. You just had to sit at the neighbor's house and do nothing."

"But I was a little boy then."

"Right—and now you are taller. And probably you move away fast if there is a female who really gets close to you. That way you make sure that she won't walk out on you, too. You walk away first. Then you can feel noble and convince yourself that if she stayed close to you she'd probably end up getting hurt anyway."

"You didn't have to say that," Rob said from between clenched teeth, as he turned away from me. He shifted and reshifted his position as if his thoughts were somehow discomforting.

"Who is she?" I asked after a few moments.

"I didn't say there is a 'she,' " he muttered.

"Who is she?" I repeated.

"Jolie."

"Pretty?"

"Very!"

"And Jolie is . . ." and I waited for him to finish my sentence.

He leaned back in the chair and closed his eyes. A half-smile flitted at the corner of his mouth, and the frown lines softened, his breathing deepened. "Jolie is fantastic. The most special girl I know. She is unique. She is a giver—she never stops giving."

"And what does she ask of you?"

"Only that I be her friend."

"You can't handle that?"

"I don't know. I just don't know."

"Let me get this straight, you spend your time running away from a girl you obviously like because of a reason you don't know?"

"What makes you say I run away from her?"

"Because I recognize a runner when I see one."

"Realistically, things haven't always turned out great for me in the game of love. Let's face it, in love I almost *always* lose! I do not want to see her hurt. I will not hurt her!"

"How does she feel about that?"

"Oh, she thinks that neither of us has to be hurt. But she's a romantic and she looks at things with different eyes than I do."

"I certainly hope so. If the two of you view things exactly alike, then one of you is unnecessary! One of the great things about men being men and women being women is the differences . . . *and,* their sameness. One of the great things about men being men and women being women is Man and Woman!

"And, by the way, O Eternal Pessimist, Jolie is right—neither of you *has* to be hurt."

"It would have to end sometime," and Rob's voice lowered with each word as if what he had just said was inevitable and the very thought was causing him more distress than he could handle.

"I see. So you end it now and never know the joy, the discovery, the completeness. You know, Rob, there is a distinct possibility that the azalea in my front yard will die at some time. Instead of protecting it, caring for it, or treasuring it, perhaps I should cut it down before it blooms, before I thrill at its beauty, before it has a chance to be."

"You certainly aren't making my position any easier."

"I sincerely hope not!"

"Oh, Ginilou, what can I say? Jolie makes me feel like a somebody. She listens to me, she cares, she makes me feel good. And I know that if I'd only let her she'd give me all those words that I've ever wanted to hear."

"Are you counting on her always being a part of your life?"

Rob hit the arm of his chair with the palm of his hand. His eyes flashed and his voice was dangerously soft, the words clipped. "Look, there aren't any strings. I place no demands or restrictions on her. Granted, I think she has put some on herself because of the way she feels, but I haven't asked her to! If she should find another man who is right for her, I'd be the very first to give her my congratulations!"

"Right, I understand. Now, are you counting on her always being there?"

Sigh . . .

"I suppose I am," he said as he shrugged his shoulders. "Besides," he added in an attempt to change the subject and lighten our conversation up a bit, "I like looking at her! And I really like the way she makes me feel when she looks at me!"

"I see."

"I know what you're trying to say! You're trying to tell me that I'm a fool, aren't you? You're saying that someday when I pick up the telephone and call her she'll say, 'Too late, pal.' That's what you're saying, isn't it?"

"No."

"Yes, it is."

"No."

"Why not? You might as well. I know it's true! It's bound to happen. Do you know that sometimes I wake up in the night, scared because I've dreamed that I called her and she's gone!"

"And have you told her?"

"No. I can't. Not yet."

"Rob, if you care, tell her. She doesn't ask you for things you cannot say—just tell her the things that you *can* say that make a difference.

"If you love (or whatever word you're using for it),

> if it's real,
> if you feel it—
> then *say* it!

It's important!

It may not change your fears.

In fact, it probably won't.

And it may not alter the facts.

But it will live and glow
> and brighten the corners
> of an otherwise
> dull, dreary world.

It will give you a song to sing,

    a dream to dream,
      a step to match your own.
  And, when time is over,
      one regret won't be yours—
  'I never told her that I loved her.' "

There was silence for a moment, and when I looked over at Rob there seemed to be a slight glint of moisture in his eyes. When he finally spoke his tone was soft and gentle, "Ginilou, did you tell *him?* A lady doesn't wear a silver bracelet with a paperclip on it unless it's something special."

The silver bracelet and its paperclip never leave my wrist.

In a room full of people in festive holiday glow, with everyone spouting well wishes—even to people they didn't like—he playfully tossed me the paperclip and mouthed the words, "Merry Christmas."

In these jaded times when love is doubted and mistrusted, when touch is shunned, where emotions are to be denied, and my own self-worth is usually three points lower than nil, it is unbelievably important that I know that "once upon a time" there was a man who looked at me and cared. The paperclip is a constant, visible reminder that even should it never happen again, there *was* a man—a man who cared about me.

"Yes, I told him. He didn't want to believe me. He's tried to erase it from his memory. But yes, I told him."

There was a long pause before Rob spoke again. "Ginilou, it's very important to me that I know. When the day finally comes that he wants to hear those words again from you, will you be there to tell him?"

"Yes," I whispered.

"I'll tell Jolie tonight."

Later, as the flight attendant cleared away our snack trays, Rob tilted his chair back and slowly admitted, "You know, in my work I see so many women who appear to me to be no more than a human shell filled to overflowing with distrust and hatred of all men."

"Ummm. And I find myself sitting here next to a man who is filled to overflowing with distrust and hatred of women."

"Point for you! However, in my defense, let me say that I don't distrust just women. The simple fact is, I don't trust many people—men or women."

"Me neither. Trust is not automatic."

"But I haven't heard you sound bitter."

"Of course I am bitter. If you look deep enough I am a lot of things! As for my not automatically hating all men, I was reared by my mother and several exceptionally good men—my grandfather, my dad, and my Uncle Frank—to be man-oriented."

"You and your dad must be very close."

"Always have been."

The summer we moved to Boston, we had to stop over in Pittsfield for a week because Dad had agreed to conduct the state youth camp.

One hot afternoon, a man who was helping out at the camp decided that he would teach me to swim. He happened to have a doctor's degree, but his common sense was about the size of half a shriveled green pea. He threw me into the lake where the water was well over my head, and then he stood there on the dock with his hands on his hips and a smile on his lips, waiting for me to "swim."

But I didn't swim. I sank just like a little rock—down and down.

There wasn't any doubt about it—I was drowning. When fear had crushed my ribs and terror had exploded through my brain, all of a sudden I felt two strong arms around me. And I knew my daddy had hold of me!

I stopped my struggling 'cause I knew, without the shadow of a doubt, no matter how long it would take to get to the top, everything was gonna be OK 'cause my daddy had hold of me!

Years later I lay on the dock at my parents' home at nightfall. The moon's reflection played on the smooth surface of the lake. I felt tears slide down my cheeks and watched as they dimpled the face of the lake. Here I was—misunderstood, misquoted, ugly, unloved, unwanted— and I felt like I was drowning. I pushed my cheek against the rough boards of the dock, closed my eyes, and clenched my teeth in an effort to stop the spinning sensation in my head. Settling over me like a warm security blanket came the remembrance of my dad's strong arms as he carried me to the life-restoring air above the water's surface. *Hey, world—take another look!*

I ain't through yet! I'm not gonna quit!

A grin tingled its way through my body and I began to hum "Jesus Got Ahold of My Life and He Won't Let Me Go!"

For no particular reason, I thought of my great-grandfather. When I was about four years old, the boy next door, J.T., careened down the uneven, slate slab sidewalk at a high run, bumped into me and sent me and my lil' red tin bucket full of milk sailing across the walk and into the ditch by the road. J.T. didn't even glance back. I picked myself up, along with my now-empty bucket, and crawled out of the ditch onto the sidewalk.

Grandpa appeared beside me and with his snow white handkerchief, which, it seemed to me, was at least half as big as a bedsheet and smelled of cedar, wiped the dirt off my face and the blood off my knees.

"Baby-chile, you're OK!" he told me confidently. "You'll always be just fine long as you remember to get up one more time than you're knocked down."

Hey, Grandpa! I'm up again.

9:00 P.M.

"Ginilou, since you have admitted that there is such a thing as being in love with love, do you realize that what you're saying is that there is real love and counterfeit love?"

"Well, let me tell you—I grew up surrounded by love. The real stuff, not counterfeit. I have never seen any two people more full of love nor more perfectly matched than my parents. I have never heard them fight. Don't get me wrong, they do have differences of opinion. They just don't fight about them. I have never seen either of them stalk off in a snit and pout, nor seen a disgusted, disgruntled, belittling look pass between them. They are both masters in the art of sarcasm, but I have never heard them use that sharp knife on each other. The house was, and is, filled with love and joy, and lots of touching, laughing, working, talking, and sharing. Now, if any kid should have grown up able to recognize real love, it's that awkward, big-eyed young'un who observed love at first hand, from the very first moment of life, every day throughout the years. Would you agree?"

"Sure! Seems so to me!"

"Ummm. Now it's storytime. Rob, let's say that as a child your parents came to you and told you about orange juice."

"Orange juice?" Rob asked incredulously.

"Orange juice. They held up a pitcher full of that brightly colored elixir and before your very eyes they slowly poured a glassful. You watched as it overflowed the rim of the pitcher and you listened to the sound as it splashed and slid up the sides of the glass. You noticed it is thicker than water and somehow richer-looking. You stuck your chubby little finger in the glass and wiggled it about to feel the texture, and when you put your finger in your mouth to lick it clean, you were joyously surprised at the sweetness. You believed your parents when they told you that it would satisfy your thirst.

"Later, a pretty young thing stood before you and poured for you a glass of bright orange liquid.

"It poured like orange juice, it sounded like orange juice, it felt like orange juice, it was sweet like orange juice—but it wasn't orange juice! It was Tang!

"So you continued on your search and over the years you have become quite cynical and totally convinced that perhaps there were only two real oranges ever made . . . and the whole world is full of Tang!

"Tang, Tang everywhere, and not one drop of real orange juice for you.

"Then, if you're lucky, one day, weary of the search, convinced of its futility, and bitter about what you feel is life's cruel joke, you receive from the hand of a close friend, a frosty glass, brimful of frothy liquid. You raise it to your lips and glory, hallelujah! *Orange juice!*"

After a few silent seconds Rob cleared his throat. "Ginilou, you're the only person I know who could make me feel emotional over a glass of orange juice, but you have made your point. Tell me this, do you think that everyone who has a marriage that isn't working just simply doesn't have real 'orange juice,' so to speak?"

"No, I don't. Some people have the makings of the real thing, but they simply aren't willing to strain out the seeds or to stop watering-it-down. Some people are so self-centered—so spoiled, lazy, and immature—that they wouldn't invest the time to lift out the seeds if you handed them a spoon."

"What do you suppose destroys it?"

"Real love? Nothing! You can decide to walk away from it, you can throw it away, but it isn't destroyed. If you have a gold piece you can decide you don't want it anymore; you can let it become tarnished and you can decide you're finished with it and toss it over your shoulder and out the window. But there it is and there it stays, real gold lying in the mud."

"So real love lasts?"

"Yes. Forever. Take Elizabeth and Jerry, for example. They are special people of love. They are two people who chose to walk with me through dark nights filled with the dragons of persecution and jealousy and the disease-carrying vampires of falsehood. If I live to be 492 I'll never be able to adequately thank Jerry and Liz for their caring support and love.

"Elizabeth is one of the truly beautiful people. She is gorgeous beyond belief. She is the only person I know who can be sick as a duck and still look lovely. I, on the other hand, can get half a sniffle and I look like week-old pizza! When she was very young, Elizabeth fell in love with and married Bruce. Years later, he died.

"Jerry is one of the 'salt-of-the-earth' people. He possesses a loyalty beyond question to those he cares about—a quality rarely seen these days. While very young, he fell in love and married Thelma. Years later, she died.

"Elizabeth and Jerry, in due time, grew in love and married. And it's refreshing and beautiful to see! Now, their respective love for Bruce and Thelma was not destroyed. It lasts—not as a club to hold over each other's head, but as an ongoing affirmation that love is!"

"That's marvelous! Your friends are lucky!"

"Yep, and blessed! My dear Rob, real love shines and spills over. Its sweetness fills the cracks of humdrumidity. It lasts. It satisfies. It tickles and delights. And sometimes it slips up on you and catches you totally unaware!"

I know her as well as it's possible to know someone. In the "mirror of self" I glimpse her. She walked wide-eyed with measured steps—a loser in love, used by life—encased by a confining shell to shield her from ever being hurt. There were those who tried to pierce that shell. But she always walked away with no loss of emotion.

One day, bone-weary, she rested on a street curb and warmed herself in the winter noonday sun. She lazily watched the passers-by as they tramped along, looking at each display of life's Art Festival. She heard a familiar voice say, "Wanna share my sandwich? How about a sip of my Pepsi?" She looked up into friendly, crinkly eyes, and for the first time she felt truly warm. With wonder, she marveled that somehow the shell had cracked and disappeared. "No, thank you," she whispered, because she didn't want anything to intrude and cause her to lose the moment's soft, newborn awareness.

Later, in the marshmallowy semidarkness of her home, she let her fingers gently turn the dial of the telephone and when the familiar voice said, "Hello?" she softly said, "How long have you known that I'm in love with you?"

"I didn't know," he said.

"I am," said she. And so she was.

Love does not keep the bad away—it is not a magic potion. But it *is* a transforming amulet. The years have come and gone and she has had to walk through varying degrees of disappointment and endure people who have attempted to use her and misuse her. Life has not always been easy. But through it all there is at the core of her very being something real to hold on to. Love, real love, lasts. It surrounds her, protects her

self-image, and enables her to open her mouth
and share, even though at times she's scared
spitless. In the face of everything—no matter
what—real love lasts!

I remember hearing a Special Someone say to
me, "Everyone needs someone to love, someone
to care about, someone special." And I hoped I
was that Special Someone for him. I wanted to
be! But I was too scared to say so!

That night, alone in my bed, still feeling warm
in the glow of "someone cares," I wondered
about all those people who have no one to make
a difference. I spoke in the darkness to the
shadows, "Everyone needs someone, but just
what if there is no someone?" The thought
stubbornly hung there, gloating, in the air and
would not go away.

So I pulled up the sheet covering my body,
wadded it up under my chin, and closed my eyes.
But it didn't help.

In my mind, I frantically darted from memory
to memory, seeking help. I happened to land
where mother was reading to me from Eger-
myers' *Bible Storybook* and I heard her say, "And
lo, I am with you always."

Suddenly everything fell into place like pieces
of an intricate mosaic. I released my grip on the
sheet bunched at my neck and stretched out my
legs and wiggled my toes. A long, long time ago,
in Bethlehem of Judea, among very unusual
circumstances, a scared little girl gave birth to a
beautiful baby boy child. And he was born to
bring a better way, a greater love, so that from

that moment on everyone would know, beyond a shadow of a doubt, they were someone special and that they were loved. "I am with you always."

"Everyone needs somebody to love."

I know, and I do.

"Ginilou, are there a lot of things in your life that you regret?"

"Reckon I'd have to know what you mean by 'a lot.' I suppose all of us would do some things differently if we knew goin' in what we know comin' out."

"Wonder why it is that we do such stupid things?"

"My dad has a 'scripture' that covers that. Perhaps I should tell you that his first name is Al. Anyway, he says, 'St. Albert 1:1—People are dumber than anybody.' "

"I've been dumb about some things. And I sincerely regret some things, but, at the time, how was I supposed to know? I should not have married Beth, but how was I supposed to know? I should have realized there was a Jolie some-where, but how was I supposed to know? And now, just maybe, it's too late. There are too many ghosts, too much water under the bridge, too many people who wouldn't understand. Jolie is *so* different. Why, my partners' wives would chew her up and have her for breakfast. I don't want to see her hurt . . ."

"And?"

"And, I'd rather have her end our friendship now before it gets to the 'let's get married' stage.

Truly, I don't want her hurt, and I honestly don't think I'll ever marry again."

"Why?"

"For years I felt that if anything should ever happen between Beth and me, I'd probably never marry again. There comes a time in your life, Ginilou, when it's just too late to start all over again. Just too late."

"Rob, I am sure that speech would get you a lot of cheers and points *somewhere*, but not from me! I'm the wrong person to tell that to! I'm a great believer in starting again—both personally and professionally. I have to believe it—I've done it, I'm *doing* it. Even if it's painful, even if people don't understand, I have to believe that it's *never* too late to start again!"

"Oh, Ginilou, how I want to believe that!"

"Rob, there is absolutely nothing like being in love. Nothing! Relax—enjoy it! It's love! It's time to make all those joyous discoveries about each other that only two people in love are free to experience. Savor each moment, treasure each touch, delight in each word, each sigh, each look. It's *love!* So many people just sit on the bank and dabble their feet in the river of love. Don't you know how privileged you are? Here you are, where you've dreamed of being! Oh, you . . . you . . . you *idiot!*"

"Careful, there, Ginilou. That's 'you idiot, sir'!"

"Right, Sir Idiot! Have you ever wondered what it would be like to own the largest blackboard in the word, but no chalk? Have you ever wondered what it would be like to own the Atlantic Ocean, but no boat? Have you ever wondered what it would be like to own the world's most beautiful theater, but have no audience? Well, have you?"

"Uhhh, to tell you the truth, no. But that would be horrible; most excruciating!"

"Yeah, sort of like being in love with the most fantastic girl in the world and not knowing it!"

"Ginilou, you play rough!"

"Sir Idiot, I do not 'play' at all."

"Somehow, I had figured that out!" Rob said quietly. He was silent for a few minutes, then started speaking in a soft tone.

"You know, when I first saw Jolie I just could not take my eyes off her! Realistically, I know that by some standards she isn't a great beauty. Yet, to me, there isn't a more beautiful woman on earth. Her eyes, her laugh, her spirit—just her. She's totally gorgeous! There is some indefinable something within her that makes her the most desirable of females to me! I simply can't explain it, but if I live forever and a day I'll never be over Jolie. No matter how things turn out, or what happens, there will always be, for me, Jolie! Nothing, no one, can ever take away from me what she has given to me, what she means to me. The first time I ever kissed her, it was so . . . so . . . I don't know, sort of like a couple of kids. It was . . ."

"It was pure."

"Yes. How did you know?"

"Because, once upon a time I had a kiss just like that and I'll never quite be over that kiss—or him."

"Say, Ginilou, is kissing important to you?"

"Is Kermit green?"

"That important?"

"That important!"

Kisses have always been important to me, even as a child.

Uncle Sam would grab me and toss me in the air. He would "whisker" me and tickle me till I would be weak with laughing and limp from trying to escape. Then he'd gently kiss me on the neck and hold me so tightly that I could scarcely breathe.

My great-grandpa would be sitting on the front porch and as our car would start down the lane each summer in July, I'd see him shade his eyes with his left hand and I knew he was saying, "Mommie, I think it's them!"

The gate would squeak, the slate walk would be slanted, a breeze would be blowing through the trees. It would be cool in the shade. The bright faces of the zinnias in the sunshine would be dripping with color as true as the little blocks of watercolors in a child's black metal paint box.

Great-Grandpa, smelling of a mixture of sunshine and tobacco, would hold me tightly to him, his long white beard cushioning my cheek. He would kiss me on the forehead, his blue eyes would fill with tears, and ever so easily he'd pat my head, run his hand down the length of my hair, and whisper against my forehead, "My child, my child . . . my own."

Granddaddy never kissed me in the conventional way, at least that I remember. He'd hold me close, nibble the top of my ear, "puff" on my forehead, or pinch my cheek. Granted, it was different—but it was a kiss.

And, of course, my daddy's kisses—never thought of in descriptive terms. They were, and are, simply "Daddy's kisses"—full of love and always identifiably his.

Jim kissed me—my first real boy-girl kiss. The day had been full of marvelous things like riding through the park on a day too hot for bike riding, watching a ball game, and staring at the old men bowling on the green. We ate hot dogs and shared a frozen custard.

The sun went down and hand-in-hand we walked across the little wooden bridge and sat down on the grass by the stream. The heat of the day left my skin tingling. Sounds—giggles from the older kids and music from the bandshell—seemed so far away. The lights blinked on throughout the park and nothing was said.

Jim put his arm around me. I shivered, and then he kissed me. A quick little hard smack on the lips and it was over. In a voice too high he said, "Guess we'd better go home."

I sat on the crossbar as we rode home—I was blushing and sure that everyone could see the kiss perched there on my lips.

My first real kiss . . .
the beginning.
There have been many others—
kisses of "friendship,"
desire,
even hate.
A kiss to start a marriage,

A kiss to say "good-bye,"
A kiss to ease the hurt.
And your kiss, friend,
a "pure" kiss.
A kiss of love, passion, life—
And the day was right and life was good.
Ah, but that was yesterday.

9:05 P.M.

"It seems to me, Ginilou, that as I look back at them, my regrets, my disappointments, really were not big things. Most of the time they were just a collection of little disappointments that somehow mushroomed into huge regrets.

"I am such a sucker for a sob story! I get too involved too quickly. Then because I hate to hurt anyone, I sort of half-heartedly play whatever role the person wants for me until I can get myself untangled from the whole thing. By that time, I totally regret the relationship and find myself pulling away from everyone and everything for a while. Then, along comes some other sob story that catches me unaware, and there I go again!"

"Rob, what was it that attracted you to Jolie?"

"When I first met Jolie, something about her made me want to protect her. Life hadn't been all that kind to her and I had the feeling that she was really in danger of letting life destroy her. I just wanted to put my arms about her and shield her from anything that would hurt her. Later—much, much later—I found out she really didn't need my protection! She can take care of herself."

"Poor Jolie."

"What do you mean by that?"

"Apparently Jolie is a survivor."

"She is!"

"And because she is, you decide she doesn't need your protective hand? Once upon a time, my best friend watched me go through a terribly rough period of time, and after the dust was settling he said to me, 'I used to worry about you, but not anymore! I know now that you can take care of yourself!' How unfair! Of course I can take care of myself! In the words of a once-popular song, 'I will survive.' But how dare he not know that I needed his support and encouragement to provide me with that added bit of 'starch' for my backbone to eventually carry me through?

"I am a survivor. I will make it! But that does not mean that I don't need a somewhere, a someone, who will help me put aside my survivor's shell and—hidden from prying eyes—let me rest my battered, bleeding soul, and replenish my ebbing strength from a mutual well, brimful of cool, refreshing, genuine care. Because, believe me, I do need that!"

"Jolie knows that I care, even though I don't actually tell her. She knows."

"Oh, Rob, she knows only if you tell her.

Otherwise, she only suspects, or dreams, or wishes. If you hurt, Jolie is to rush over with Band-Aids for your wounded ego, and even handle major surgery if needed. If she hurts, according to you, it teaches her how to be 'independent.' A strange dichotomy, Sir Idiot."

"Ginilou, you are not very kind!"

"Right! But as you said, the little disappointments that turn into big regrets? Well, sir, I have had to handle my share and then some. And, like Jolie, I have survived. But I have news for you: survivors are not always kind! You see, we don't have a great deal of room or time for superficial kindness inside that shell we've been forced to build around ourselves in order to survive."

He promised he'd call on Friday, but he didn't— so Friday never arrived for me. Like Easter morning and the promise of a baby rabbit . . . but that year Easter didn't arrive for me.

Like New Year's Day and playing a solo with the orchestra if I learned the "Pathetique" (and I did learn it). But that year New Year's Day didn't arrive for me. Like Christmas Day and the promise of starting anew "if you'll just be patient and not rock the boat" (I did try). But that year Christmas Day never arrived for me.

The baby rabbit, playing the "Pathetique," starting over, love, and Friday's telephone call join all the things that never happen.

Tiny disappointments. Agonizing regrets!

Inside my carefully constructed shell I can have no time for the jagged pieces of broken dreams, disillusionment, regrets. To try to glue back together all the fragments of shattered rainbows would take forever. And, in the whole world, there isn't a pot of Elmer's Glue large enough to coat each tiny bit. As I grit my teeth and sadly sweep out all the slivers, I stop, pick up a couple of cracked pieces, and tuck them away for later remembering and contemplation. How fortunate that God did not require us to put it all back together in some large celestial scrapbook for later editing! How marvelous he did not require us to be perfect creatures, all alike! He made only one supreme requirement: love one another.

"And now I will show you the most excellent way. If I speak in the tongues of men and of angels, but have not love, I am only a resounding gong or a clanging cymbal" (1 Corinthians 12:31–13:1, NIV).

I can handle that. Hallelu!

9:10 P.M.

"Ginilou, anyone ever tell you that you have a strange way of talking?"

"Strange?"

"Yes, not strange-bad, but strange-wondrous. You have a fascinating way with word pictures and your use of slang intrigues me!"

"Reckon I do use a lot of slang. Once upon a time when I was but a tyke, a relative of mine almost choked to death when she overheard my cousin Pauline and me say 'Gosh!' According to her, people who used slang were quite illiterate and most of them, she thought, used slang when they really wanted to curse. It's amazing to me the people who still hold on to that same idea. If I wanted to curse instead of saying 'Great Gizzard,' I believe I know the words!

"I've even heard it said that some people use slang 'cause their vocabulary isn't sufficient. Yet I am told that my vocabulary is quite adequate.

So much for that theory. I have, upon occasion, listened as someone belabored some stupid, erroneous theory and bored me out of my skull. I could have said, 'I find the aforementioned laboriously presented ideas worthy of a position in the dumpster behind the 7-Eleven Store.' Instead, I simply shake my head and say, 'Banana seeds!' "

" 'Banana seeds'?" Rob sputtered.

"Banana seeds."

"Well, no doubt about it, that does say it better! But tell me something else. I get the idea that you talk with God on the same terms."

"I reckon so, yes."

"I just don't think that I could manage to sit down in the same room with God and just have a normal, casual conversation. I'd be too afraid that if I talked to him like I think, or even like I'm talking to you, he'd strike me with a bolt of lightning and tell me never to be disrespectful again!"

"Oh, but I am not disrespectful, Rob! While my talk may seem to you a bit unconventional, let me assure you that it positively is not disrespect-ful, or any less meaningful!"

When I wasn't much more than peanut-sized, I was scrunched up in one of my very favorite places—under Mother's desk in the living room. Zelda was standing in front of the heat register warming her backside, and my mother was knitting me a sweater for Christmas (which I wasn't supposed to know). I listened as she explained to Zelda that God always spoke to the people of every age in language that they could understand.

As I grew up, I kept trying different faces on God. I'd get in a "proper" position and get all my "proper" thees and thous all collected in my head, and then invariably I'd end up stammering and stuttering and feeling embarrassed.

Years later we lived in Niagara Falls, New York, and Zelda was visiting. Mom was knitting me a sweater for Christmas, and Zelda was counting stitches for a scarf she was knitting while warming her backside in front of the stove. And once again Mom got around to saying, "God speaks to every person in ways that he understands." And I turned over on the couch and went to sleep dreaming about the sleigh ride coming up tomorrow night.

Then it was years later and Mom and Dad lived in Detroit, Michigan, and Zelda was visiting. I had driven up from Toledo for the evening. Mom was knitting me a white sweater for Christmas, and Zelda was standing before the fireplace warming her backside. This time when Mom said that God speaks in a language people understand, this time I got it!

So I put on my coat and I walked out the back door. My shoes scrunched as I walked through the snow. I went over to Lady's pen and let myself inside. Lady was a beautiful red Irish setter and we were very fond of each other, so she didn't seem to mind that I had disturbed her warm sleep. She just huddled against me while I rubbed her velvet ears and I leaned against her dog house. "Lady," I said, "we're gonna try somethin'." I paused, and then went on. "Well, God, here we are—Lady 'n me. I doubt that she has any trouble at all communicating with you, but I've had a dab of a problem in that very area. You see, I really don't need you to be a Father to me. You already gave me the best father there is. And I don't need you to be all stiff and proper and shoutin' at me.

"Now it isn't that I don't know that you are there. And it isn't as if I haven't tried to keep lines of communication open, 'cause you know that I have. It's just that, being the dumb kid that I am, it's taken me all this time to understand that you speak to everyone in a language he understands! Since that is true, I reckon it's perfectly OK with you if I speak to you in my kind of words. And now that I understand that, I just thought I'd take time to let you know that I sure feel a lot better about talkin' to you. Later, God."

Lady licked my cheek as I whispered "Good night" against her silky head. I had closed the gate, shoved my cold hands deep into my pockets, and started back through the snow toward the house when it seemed I heard, "Hey, kid! Aren't you gonna let me speak?"

And while I laughed aloud and felt all good inside, my heart heard, "This is more like it. It's about time!"

9:15 P.M.

"Rob, does it seem to you that we've been on the ground a lot longer than the fifteen minutes they said that this stop would take?"

"That's only because we've been here thirty-five minutes!"

"Wonder what's wrong?"

"Haven't the foggiest! But I do wish that baby would stop crying."

"Maybe he's just tired."

"I'm tired, too. Of his crying!"

The intercom crackled and the flight attendant's professional-sounding voice informed us that we would be detained a while longer due to a difficulty concerning the weather and flight patterns but that it was nothing to be concerned about. They would be around momentarily with coffee and Danish.

"Ginilou, what's wrong that that baby? He's holding his head at a peculiar angle."

"Yes, I see."

"Is he OK? Drat! His crying is getting on

everyone's nerves! Where are you going? Hey! Don't bring that baby over here!"

I stood in the aisle looking at the baby's mother, a small woman who was so visibly tired it seemed as if her bones could not possibly hold her upright one moment longer. I touched her on the arm.

"Hi," I said. "Can I help? My name is Ginilou and I'd be happy to hold the baby for you so that you can get some rest. I promise to watch him carefully, and if he should start to choke I know what to do and I'll notify you immediately. I promise! Does he have a fever?"

"No," she responded, her voice so soft I could barely hear her, "No, not right now. We're on our way to Children's Hospital in Boston, and I *am* tired. His name is Josh and he is two and a half months old. If you're sure he wouldn't be a bother . . ."

"I'm sure. You rest now and don't worry. We'll be fine."

I took the crying infant from her arms as a flight attendant appeared. "Can I help?" she asked.

"Yes, you can get the mother a glass of milk and a pillow. And please, would you bring me a pillow, too?"

As I settled into my seat I said, "Rob, this is Joshua and he is two and a half months old. Josh, this is Rob and he is a bit older."

The flight attendant brought the pillow and Rob asked where to put it.

"Under your head and over your ears, if you can! I didn't say that I'd stop the baby's crying. I only said I'd hold him for a while and let his mother rest. So you'd best make yourself as comfortable as possible under the circumstances.

"Well, baby Josh," I whispered against his soft downy head, "here we are. My name is Ginilou, and I am not going to joggle, jiggle, jostle, or bounce you. I'm just going to whisper to you and hum you some songs. I'll massage your aching spine and rub your cramping legs, and—if you want to—you can stop crying. I'll be here."

I carefully placed his head so he wouldn't choke. I turned him so his little tummy was against my body and put his tiny hand flat against my skin so he could feel my heartbeat.

"Lord Jesus," I prayed, "you held the little children on your knee and said of such are the kingdom of heaven. Here's Josh. He's one of your kids, too. Please . . . help."

I began to rub Josh's back and legs and hum him lullabies that my mother had sung to me when I was a child. His eyes fanned shut, his breathing stabilized—he was asleep.

"Oh, Joshua! Sweet, sweet Joshua! I have a baby girl at home. Only she isn't a little baby anymore. Just my baby. And when she was born, Josh, she was very ill too, and no one knew whether or not she would live. But she kept on breathing. What a joy she is! Of course, there are times when she cannot breathe well and when her eyes are too big, and too dark, and her skin is chalky white. At those times I am so scared and I hold her close, just like I'm holding you now."

Jesus loves me
this I know,
for the Bible tells me so.
Little ones to Him belong,
they are weak, but He is strong
Yes, Jesus loves you (Joshua),
Yes, Jesus loves you,
Yes, Jesus loves you,
The Bible tells me so.

"I sing to her while I hold her a little ditty I made up while holding her in the hospital when she was two days old:

"My pretty little girl, my Autumn Dawn;
My pretty little baby girl, my Autumn Dawn—
She's got
   two brown eyes,
   'n a little button nose,
   a mouth to say 'I love you,'
   'n ten wiggly toes.
Lookin' at me so coy,
She's my pride and joy!
She's got
   two brown eyes
   'n a little button nose,
   a mouth to say 'I love you,'
   'n ten wiggly toes.
That's my Autumn Dawn!"

Not exactly a great song, but it keeps us going when fear settles in a big knot in the center of me and threatens to rule my life . . . The winter Autumn Dawn was four, she had an especially hard time. One illness just seemed to stretch into

the next and she grew pale and still paler, and
sometimes she didn't have energy enough to
move . . . After one long week during which sleep
was stolen in "catnaps," her sister Stormi went
out on the lake and wrote a letter to God.

Sometimes there's anger—
    gripping anger—
And I cry out in desperation,
    "How long, O Lord . . . how long?"
And there are times when I am bitter, Father,
    for it's so unfair, it seems to me,
    that one so young should be so ill.
And, Lord, I cry
    "How long . . . how long?"
You gave this gift of life when the world was
    crumbling around my mother's feet.
She was crushed and hurt and lost at the time,
    and it did not seem like a "gift" back then.
It was yet another hurt to bear
    for a woman of forty
    left alone—
    by a man who just walked out the door.
Back then it was also
    "How long . . . how long?"
    But Mother found the strength inside,
    and sensitivity was not lost to tears.
She had
    her two daughters—
        one sixteen, one eighteen years old—
    and her parents who were pillars of
        support and pride and Christian love.
And the shock that *life* was growing
    inside of her!

And I—I was sixteen and I was thrilled!
　　I said a "Thank you, Lord!"
　　For what would add sparkle to Mother's
　　　　eyes like the *joy* of a little child!
And so she came—our Autumn Dawn
　　so small
　　a beauty
and we were family.
　　Three daughters now,
　　a mother growing strong,
　　and grandparents proud.

Four years have passed
　　and, Lord, the joy she has given us.
　　　　The laughter and hugs,
　　　　the sticky fingers,
　　　　the questioning brown eyes,
　　　　　　the running
　　　　　　　　swinging
　　　　　　　　　　crying
　　　　　　　　　　　　hugging
　　　　the *love*, dear Lord—
　　　　the love she has brought us!
But God, her strength still does not stay.
　　Our Autumn Dawn grows tired—
　　　　some days are weary ones for this child
　　　　and fever mounts.
I cry in anger,
　　"How long, O Lord . . . how long?
　　You cannot take her from me now!"
Lord, I hold this child, my sister—
　　precious gift of love—
　　her body warm, too warm.
Mother and I have so often cast

a worried glance in each others' eyes.
For there are times when we simply
do not know
if she is ours to keep
or if, Lord, you would wish her
    to play inside your house—
    to wipe sticky fingers on your robe
    to play the "plano" and fill your
    world with Autumn songs.
And though I still cry in desperation,
"How long, O Lord . . . how long?"
I trust you, Father (I am trying to),
and really do accept your will.
But, Lord, O Lord, she's such a joy.
And Father, listen to my plea . . .
    Promise me you'll hold her gently
    in your arms and smile at gazing
    wondering eyes, and tell her stories
    to make her smile.
    And Lord, perhaps you'll have a swing
    like the one hanging from our huge
    oak tree built with love by our
    grandfather's steady hand.
Lord, can she run in sand,
    pick yellow daisies,
    play by fruit trees?
Do you have a grandmother to make
    her clothes,
    and mint tea, sassafras,
    and homemade bread?
And what of a mother
    to hold her at night
    and sing to her softly?
A mother who paints her toenails pink

and sculpts in clay
and paints and sings?
And Father, can you make a ponytail?
Do you have a sprinkler in your garden?
(She loves to feel the water so.)
O Father, please hear me,
please let me know.
Lord, promise me, if it be your will
that here she'll stay.
Let me never push her love away
or be too busy
to stop
and play
and run . . .
to hug . . .
to hold.
Let the family stay close,
as we are this day,
loving and laughing.
Give us wisdom and patience.
Give us strength for tomorrow.
Thank you for family—
for our love for each other
Thank you, dear Father!
That's my sister,
Father God, hold her gently . . .
please.
Hold her gently!

"Ginilou?"
"Yes, Rob?"
"He is so quiet now. Is he just sleeping?"
"Yes."
"The two of you make quite a picture there!

I've seen a lot of women holding babies, but watching you with Josh—well, I guess I've never seen a woman *really* hold a baby before."

"Oh, Rob, he's going to have to be a very strong little person, and his mother is going to need extra stamina in the time to come. I just hope they both make it."

"Your little girl, you said she was sick when she was born. *She* made it."

"Yes, up to now. But one never knows, Rob. It's just one day at a time. While the sun shines, we laugh and love, touch and hold. And then, when her fever runs high and her strength ebbs, we laugh and love, touch and hold, thank God for yesterday, and pray for a tomorrow."

The flight attendant appeared. "We've removed the arm rest from between the two seats beside the baby's mother and made him a bed if you want to put him down now."

"Thank you. But I promised his mother that I would take care of him while she rested. I'll just wait until she is awake before I put him down."

As the flight attendant disappeared down the aisle, Rob spoke. "Ginilou, can I be of help to them? What could I do?"

"You have to decide that, Rob. I don't know. Perhaps if an ambulance could be at the plane when it lands to take them to the hospital, or if there were money for a place for Josh's mother to stay, or a special nurse to relieve her occasionally, or specialists available to them, if needed."

"You don't think she has money?"

"Rob, her outfit is lovely—pastel, soft, with a 'well-taken-care-of' look. But one of the reasons it looks so becomingly soft and pastel and well taken care of is because it has been washed so often! Joshua's blanket is clean and soft, but one corner is slightly frayed. It certainly isn't new. No, I don't think she has money."

Before I could blink an eye, Rob was out of his seat and speaking to the flight attendant in low tones as they disappeared into the galley.

Noticing that Joshua's mother was awake, I carried him to her and settled him, still sleeping soundly, into his newly made bed. We exchanged a few whispered words and I went back to my seat.

As Rob seated himself beside me he said, "It's taken care of."

"What?"

"It's taken care of—all of it. It's all being taken care of."

"You beautiful man! But wasn't that terribly expensive?"

"It's only money, Ginilou."

"To *you* it's only money. To them it may very well be a miracle!"

"Maybe that's the way it is with miracles. I've always suspected that miracles, in all probability, were just something I didn't comprehend, or an ability I did not possess but that someone else could knowingly explain with ease."

"In other words, if you were intelligent enough to understand everything, then nothing would be a miracle."

"Yes, I think so."

"It seems to be, Rob, that if you possessed all knowledge, that in itself would be a miracle!"

As Rob chuckled he said, "OK, Ginilou, you tell me about miracles."

"Life is a miracle! Every day, every breath, is miraculous!"

During World War II we moved from Vandergrift, Pennsylvania, to Boston, Massachusetts, and seaport Boston was a totally different world compared to inland Pennsylvania. In an attempt to make Boston not visible by aircraft at night, streetlights were painted black except for one small slit at the bottom, and the top half of all car headlights were taped over. Food rationing was a problem for everyone and meat was almost nonexistent. Mock air raids were not "playtime" there, as they were in some sections of the United States; they were taken very seriously.

Servicemen from all branches of the military were everywhere in Boston, and it was safe to assume that their presence there meant they would be shipping out soon.

Among the others, Bruce Radaker and Johnny Robb, from Pennsylvania, found Boston their point of disembarkment. For the period left to them before shipping out, they spent every free moment at our apartment. Dad gave them a key so they could let themselves in and out—and that started a whole new existence for us.

From that day to VE Day, those keys passed from the hands of lonely, scared, combat-bound service boys to the cold, trembling hands of some incoming recruit.

We had to be very careful when getting out of

bed each morning 'cause you just never knew who you might step in the middle of! We often went to bed at night just the three of us—Dad, Mom, and me—only to awaken in the morning to find every available inch of floor space occupied by sleeping servicemen.

Everyone it seemed wanted a last "taste of home"—home cooking, family love and laughter, walking to church and worshiping together (even if they'd never attended church before).

At Thanksgiving, Mother stood in line at the market for hours waiting her time at the counter, and all that was available were two mackerel.

Dad "built" a dasher, attached it to our cookie crock, and Mom ladled into it the thick yellow cream she had so carefully skimmed off the milk. Then she laboriously churned real, honest-to-goodness butter. Not that lardy white stuff you were supposed to squeeze a yellow capsule through and then pretend it tasted good as you-know-what (only it never did—it always tasted like yellow-tinted lardy white stuff!).

Somewhere Dad found some cornmeal and fresh eggs and Mother baked the best cornbread in the world. Mother always bakes the best cornbread.

With a dab of this, and a squirt of that, a pinch of thus 'n so, homemade cornbread, real butter, and two stinky mackerel—Mom and Dad built a Thanksgiving for a tribe of scared, big-eyed, not quite dry-behind-the-ears little boys parading about in soldier suits.

Talk about miracles! Somehow after that,

those biblical "loaves and fishes" have never seemed all that incredible!

"I believe in miracles! I've seen too many not to believe!

"Today, Anna Mae Roberts discovered that the spot on her lung had disappeared: miraculous!

"Today, Joey Martinez managed by great inner strength to hold onto his uncontrollable temper and did not punch Michael Lee in his pearly whites: miraculous!

"Yes, indeed, I believe in miracles!"

9:25 P.M.

"Ginilou, that gold medallion on your
necklace . . ."

My fingers raised to touch the charm, "What
about it?"

"It says, 'Betty'?"

"Yes."

"Can you tell me about her?"

I turned my gaze out the window as unbidden
waves of what I do not wish to accept wash
across me. Like it or not they burst through my
brain and roar out their importance so I cannot
escape.

It all started with a telephone call.

Brrring. Brrring.

"Hello?"

"Tom is leaving Betty," came the urgent words
from the familiar voice of my closest friend who
spoke in a most unfamiliar tone.

"She'll need someone to talk with—someone
to help. I'd go if I could, but I can't. So . . ."

"So you want *me* to go?"

"Yes," he said.

"But I barely know her!"

"She's important to me."

"OK, OK, friend, I'll see what I can do. But you owe me one!"

Driving to Betty's house thoughts kept bouncing about in my brain. I wished that I knew her better. The only time I had seen her had been at church. She was a petite, vivacious, mischievous sort of woman with short dark hair and apparently a charming sense of humor. Now it seemed her marriage was dissolving as quickly as if it had been aimed at and hit by a disintegrating ray.

I parked the car and walked toward her house. *What on earth am I going to say?* I wondered. "Hello, I hear that your marriage is falling apart. How's about I come in and watch it unravel?" Perhaps not. Maybe, "Hello there, you don't know me very well, and I know you hardly at all, and I haven't the foggiest notion as to exactly why I'm here, but I just thought I'd come by and stare while you cry your peepers out." Ummm, no.

When Betty opened the door to my tentative knock, it was apparent she had been crying long and hard. Still having nothing to say, I took a deep breath, and we started our fledgling relationship with, "Hi, Betty."

"Hi, Ginilou."

"Can I . . . help?"

"No one can help!" Her face crumbled, her body shook as if with convulsions, and her long slim fingers gripped my hands so tightly they hurt. She sobbed until she was weak, then silence descended because the words were too weighty to utter.

It seemed important at the moment that she get out of that house—*their* house—where it had been the two of them, the 'us' she had thought indestructible. So I helped her pack an overnight case, put her in my car, and we drove to my house. Settling her on the couch, I escaped into the kitchen to fix some coffee.

Awkward silence had wrapped itself around us and between us in huge boulders, and there seemed to be no way to climb across them.

"Ginilou," Betty finally whispered in a water-logged voice, as I gratefully breathed a sigh of relief, "where did you get this piece of slate on your coffee table?"

"Kentucky," I answered as I handed her a cup of coffee.

"Kentucky?" Her voice seemed to brighten slightly. "You must be kiddin'!"

"Nope, I'm not. I picked it up right out of Clear Creek."

"Clear Creek?" No doubt about it this time, her voice was definitely on an upswing. "Ginilou, I'm from Mt. Sterlin'!"

"Gizzard, you must be! Anyone else would say 'Mt. Ster*ling*.' Wanna sing a chorus of 'It's a Small World'? You know, I have a whole passell of kin in Salt Lick and I spent every summer of my childhood there."

"Every summer? You don't suppose we met sometime, some summer, when we were young?" And for the next little bit we jabbered like a couple of kids about the Kentucky we shared.

We talked of standing on top of the mountains and seeing below us the curving, twisting roads appearing like a carelessly discarded bolt of white ribbon; of fields of tobacco and the furry green worms that cling on suction-cupped feet to the underneath of those huge yellow-green leaves in the *hot* summer time; of the sweet smell of bubblin' cane that laced the cool fall night air with teasing, mouth-watering thoughts of sorghum molasses; of slippin' and sliddin' across the smooth slate rock in cold mountain streams; and of the unbelievable array of autumn colors that splashed across the regal trees in fall.

For the next few months as she painfully trudged her way through separation, divorce, and the cruel speculation of gossipy people, Betty and I were never very far apart.

During that time she lost weight drastically and her face grew hard and pinched. Her laugh no longer contained the sound of a tinkling wind chime but held only bitterness and sarcasm. I watched as the vivacious, spontaneous side of Betty disappeared into nothingness and silently I mourned the loss. Helplessly I stood by as she went about the lonely and laborious task of building an invisible shield that would keep anyone from ever getting close enough to hurt her again. Like an injured animal in pain, she retreated into a hiding-place existence where only a very few were welcome—and there she stayed, seemingly for good.

Finally something inside, something known only to her, began to send forth small purrings of safety. Gradually she started gaining a little weight and her haunted look diminished a bit. One evening I looked across the supper table and noticed a glint of pure mischief in her eyes.

"Betty!" I fairly shouted. "You're in there! You really are in there!"

By then, somewhere along the way, at some indefinable point, we had become closer than most people ever become. By mutual, unspoken consent we walked through the secret rooms of each other's lives, and then carefully shut every door and softly turned the lock, knowing that what we had glimpsed was sacred and therefore we held it in complete reverence.

One night Betty paced the living room for hours pursued by the dragon named "why."

"Ginilou, why did it happen?"

"Don't know now anymore than I did four hours ago when you asked me. Some things just happen.

"I don't know why
    a heart stops beating
    when there seems to be
    . no reason;
I don't know why
    a heart stops caring
    when there seems to be
        no reason;
I don't know why
    a heart stops loving
    when there seems to be
        no reason;
I don't know *why.*
I only know

142

sometimes
it happens."

She sat on the couch and pulled her feet up under her—her eyes, too large in her small face, were filled with tears. She looked like a child waiting for the doctor to administer a shot.

"People who I thought were my best friends have pulled away from me. All of a sudden it's as if I have leprosy! Before I was a friend. Now I'm a threat!"

"Oh, Bett, some people just don't know how to handle divorce, just like some people can't be around illness. They can't handle it, they don't know how."

"Spare me! That isn't a valid reason and you know it!"

"Yep, I know."

One afternoon as I stepped out of the shower there was Betty leaning against the bathroom door.

"Good afternoon, madam," she began in a pseudoannouncer's voice, speaking into my hairbrush as if it were a microphone, "I'm an interviewer for *Fashion Magazine* and we'd be interested in knowing who designed your stunning outfit."

"It's an original," I snapped as I reached for a towel, "and it's not for sale!"

"Not even for the right price?"

As I finished drying and turned to go into the bedroom, I wiggled my eyebrows at her and demurely said, "Would a quarter be too much?"

She giggled and followed me into the bedroom. I smiled at her over my shoulder.

"You know, Bett, you are one of the earth's great gigglers. I think when God decided he'd like to design a giggle he had you in mind. You have got to be the champion of quality gigglers."

"Can I, and my giggle, stay for supper? I really don't want to be alone in that house tonight."

"Sure."

"How 'bout meatloaf for supper?"

"OK, you cut up the green peppers. I'll chop the onions."

"Gee! You actually trust me with a sharp knife?" she asked sarcastically.

"Reckon I'll have to. I really don't want to have to watch while you beat the peppers into pieces with a blunt stick!"

Betty turned on the stereo and we went about preparing our meal in silence except for occasionally humming along with some song or other.

We had nearly finished eating when Betty laid down her fork. "Ginilou, I'm so full of hate."

"I know."

"Sometimes it scares me."

"I know. Eat your peas."

Picking up her fork she pushed the peas around her plate like a six-year-old. "When *he* walked out on you—did you hate him?"

"Wasn't exactly overly fond of him!"

"Are you free of the hate now?"

"It isn't the bugaboo it once was."

"Well, I know this, I'll never be free of it and I'll never, not ever, love again."

"Yes, O Obstinate One, you will."

"It'd take a miracle."

"OK."

"OK? What's that? You just gonna whomp me a miracle out of thin blue air?"

"Maybe I'll knit you one out of a smile, and a tear, and a dream . . . and time."

"How about you knit you one, too?"

"Nope. Can't be done or I would have done it."

The next morning while pouring coffee at the breakfast table, Betty said, "My body aches. Know what I mean?"

"Yes, I know. It will."

"How long?"

"I don't know."

She started buttering a biscuit, "Is it too soon for me to go out? On a date I mean. People would talk, don't you think?"

"Do you want to go out?"

"Yes."

"Then go. 'People' don't have to walk in your shoes."

"Do you think I'm terrible?"

"Right, terrible and silly!"

"Oh, I remember them. Weren't they a vaudeville team? Terrible and Silly, and Silly played the clarinet!"

It was raining hard one evening as Betty came dashing in the front door looking more like a bedraggled pup caught out in a storm.

"It's hot chocolate time," she said as she flew into the bathroom for a towel to dry her hair.

I fixed the hot chocolate and we took our usual places in the living room—Betty at one end of the couch, me at the other, both of us leaning against the armrests with our feet up on the couch.

"This is my 'home safe,' you know, my 'All-e-all-e-in free.' Remember playing hide 'n seek? Finally the seekers would give up tryin' to find you and they'd shout 'All-e-all-e-in-free' and then you could run back and lean against the tree and be safe. Well, this is my 'home safe'—this room, all browns and wood and living plants. It's like a secret tuckaway in the forest. It's you."

"Why do you need a 'home-safe' tonight?"

"I have this fear . . . I can't seem to escape it."

"Can you put a name tag on it?"

"Yeah, I don't think I'll ever be really acceptable."

"To whom?"

"*Them* . . . people. You know. How did you come to terms with that?"

"I had to decide whether it was more important to be acceptable to the great thundering herd or to *me*. One evening after an encounter with the 'acceptable ones' I sat right here in this living room, cried out of frustration and rejection, and mentally fashioned an acceptable me. You know, two arms, two legs, two hands, two feet, two ears, two eyes, one nose, one mouth, and various other parts. From these I started designing a me that was acceptable!

"I thought, I'll need a smile. It needn't be sincere, no one will really know. Just a small acceptable smile. And I'll need a *reliable* look in my eyes—not too dumb, not too smart—just a steady reliable look. I'll need to hear the *normal* sounds—not the call of the wind, or the cry of a heart, or the whisper of a snowflake—but the everyday, normal, humdrum sounds.

"I'll need to walk the *acceptable* way, with my acceptable nose in the air and my acceptable arms at my acceptable sides and touch no one, nothing.

"I'll learn the rules, I thought, *and then from their acceptable positions perhaps one day when I walk by (in my acceptable way, and smiling my acceptable smile) the world will think its acceptable thought that it's good I have finally found such an acceptable way of living acceptably.*"

In the gathering silence Betty finally spoke in measured, quiet tones, "That would not be you!"

"Right. That's what I decided, too. And if I'm going to travel through this world, I'm gonna do it as an original. I'm part of every experience I've ever had. No one has ever met all the exact same people I have met in the very same way, nor had the exact same experiences. I am me, uniquely me. And while that may not be acceptable to some, I *am* acceptable to me and to God.

"More hot chocolate?"

"Oh no, I couldn't. I shouldn't . . . well, just a drop. A short gallon would be nice!" I refilled her cup and she settled back into the couch arm with a thoughtful look on her face.

"Remember the 'body aches' we mentioned before?" she said. "Do you have them too?"

"Sure I do. When you've been used to a satisfactory sexual relationship and then suddenly, *kachung!* it is ended—your physical, psychological, and emotional clock is turned upside down. It produces its own type of insanity, I think."

"I don't like it."

"No, neither do I."

"I could scream."

"Go ahead."

"It won't help."

"Nope, probably not. But then, it won't hurt either. So go ahead, if you've a mind to."

"If I've a mind to?"

"Sure. One night a while back, I heard Roger Miller on television singing a song called 'You Can't Rollerskate in a Buffalo Herd.' He ended it by saying, 'But you can try, if you've a mind to.' I realized it wasn't going to make the next issue of *101 Best Loved Hymns*, but it was, and is, a dandy piece of advice."

"If I have a mind to, *if* I have a mind to . . . that's really it, isn't it? If I've a mind to turn loose, to get out and meet people . . . if I've a mind to reach out, to try, to get it in gear and start movin.' If I've a mind to!"

"By George!" I said smiling, "I think she's got it!"

And Betty did have a mind to! Filling her life with forward motion, she acknowledged the past but stopped crying about it. She polished her self-image and went about daily living while searching for that illusive critter called 'happiness.' She made the painful decision to move to Sarasota to put things behind her. That's when our middle of the night marathon conversations ceased. Our communication became confined to scribbled notes on postcards and weekend visits where we'd talk nonstop into the wee hours of the night and awaken before dawn to start anew.

Once again she was vivacious, spontaneous, and vibrant. That little Kentuckian half-pint had gritted her teeth, pulled herself together, and by great determination she had survived! Yippee!

Then, one Thursday afternoon when I answered the phone, Bett's voice came singing into my ear, "I'm bringing you a visitor on Saturday."

"Who?"

"Gene. He—says he—loves me," she whispered hesitantly.

"And you? Do you love him?"

"I don't know. I don't trust love, you know I don't."

"I know."

"Please, when you meet him, tell me if you believe he loves me."

"It doesn't matter whether *I* believe it, do you believe he loves you?"

"I think so."

"Then why the hesitancy in your voice?"

"Ginilou, tell me again about love."

"Most important thing there is! Without love and care, there is nothing."

"But what *is* love. Why is it?"

"Love isn't a what or a why, love is an is! Love just is!

Grass grows and it's green.
    It comes back year after year.
    I don't know why, but it does—
    Grass is.
Jays are blue and they fly.

They come back year after year.
I don't know why, but they do—
Jays are.
True love is joy. It grows
and it lasts, year after year.
I don't know why, but it does.
Love is."

On Saturday Bett fairly bubbled into the house, a man at her side. After making introductions she zipped off to unknown places to "give you two time to get acquainted."

Self-consciously settling himself on the couch where only months earlier Betty had sobbed because "there is no such thing as love," Gene talked about his feelings for Betty. He used words like "adore" and "worship" and "cherish" and "love." He was enthusiastic about her and charmed by her, and some time during that afternoon I became a believer in his love for her.

A few months later they were married.

Shortly afterwards Betty called me one night at 11:45 P.M.

"What's wrong?" I nervously asked.

"Nothin'," she giggled. "Like ol' times, huh? We had a phone put in today 'n I couldn't wait to call! I really wanted to wait another hour or two! Guess what color the phone is?"

"Color? Why it's yellow you sun-worshiper you!"

Once again, at odd moments, my life was cheered by the magic of sharing delicious moments and secret confidences. Whenever Betty could come for a visit, time would seem to speed up. There was never sufficient time to convey everything that needed to be said. It was common for people around us to remark, "I don't understand a word those two say, they seem to be speaking in shorthand."

One Saturday I was restless and had the uncomfortable feeling that something was going to happen. The telephone rang, and when I heard her voice the jittery feelings disappeared. When I finally glanced at the clock and noticed we had been talking for well over an hour, I couldn't believe it!

"Bett, hang up and let me call you back so we can share in this expense."

"No. No," she said emphatically, "this call is mine. All mine. It's something I have to do."

It was a soft, emotional, moving conversation. If it had been a flower, it would have been a white rose. If it had been a day, it would have been a picture-perfect first snow before anyone had walked through leaving prints to mar the surface. If it had been a season, it would have been autumn.

We talked of many things—of joys, of sorrows, of love, of life, of death.

We talked of going home: "Ginilou, promise me that next summer we'll go back to Kentucky together. Please? It's important to me. Promise me that we will walk the hills together next summer."

"OK, I promise."

We talked of her parents: "If I had a heap of money I'd buy my parents a beautiful home, and I'd take them on a marvelous trip."

We talked of our mutual, special friend: "I wish

he knew you like I do. Tell him that I love him."

When it was time to hang up, neither of us seemed capable of saying, "Good-bye."

"Are you coming up soon?" I asked.

"Soon. I'll see you soon."

"Good, I miss you, Bett."

"I miss you, too. Still I always feel a part of you is with me."

"I know that feeling. Take care, Bett."

"See ya," she said.

"Bye." I slowly moved the phone from my ear, but for some unexplainable reason tears ran down my face and I couldn't place the receiver in its cradle.

"Ginilou," I heard her shout, "Hey, Ginilou!"

"Yes, Bett," I said raising the phone again to my ear, "I'm here."

"I love you. Oh, how much I love you."

> One week later, on
> > July 20,
> > Betty Jones Allen
> > > was struck dead by lightning.

I wanted to scream a shattering scream that would split here from hereafter. I wanted us to stand in a sundrenched spot atop the mountains where time stands still. I wished I had someone, *something*, to hate—to lash out against.

A drunken driver,
a doctor with an incorrect diagnosis,
research teams who work too slowly—
something,
someone
to strike out against.

In anger I jabbed my finger into the holes of

the telephone dial and with fury I turned each
number that would, I was positive, bring me the
reassuring voice of our best friend.

Brrring!
Surely he will tell me it's a cruel hoax.
Brrring!
He will say that it's a lie.
Click! The ringing stops and I hear his
voice . . . and I know.

In anguish I threw my temper tantrum and
figuratively I beat my fists against his chest. My
body was wracked with shooting pain and the
sobs would not cease.

"Please, stop crying," he said gently. "You must
stop or you'll be sick, and that isn't going to help
Betty. I know you loved her."

"Loved her? Loved? I *love* her. I *do* love her!"
"But she is gone!" he said emphatically.
Gone.
Dead.
No longer to be counted among the present.

I sent a bud vase with a single rose to her
memorial service. "I dislike large bunches of
flowers," she had said during our last telephone
conversation. "Just a single rose from someone
who loves me. Did you hear me, Ginilou?"

I heard you, Bett.

On July 22nd my daughter, Jayelynn, presented
to me the small medallion suspended from a
gold chain. Lovingly and tearfully she placed it
around my neck. "Betty—in memory."

"Ginilou?" Rob's voice abruptly interrupted my
memories. "Ginilou, are you crying?"

"No, not really," I reply, knowing that what I've said will appear foolish since there are, in fact, tears rolling down my face.

"Those *are* tears, aren't they?"

"Yes, but I'm not crying. You asked about Betty. Well, Betty was sunlight and giggles, a dancing, shimmering sprite who came into my life with the subtleness of an elephant and the quietness of a bass drum. She became a part of my very breathing. And then, suddenly, she stepped into another dimension—a place I cannot see, where I could not follow."

"I see. She died. But tell me, doesn't wearing that medallion make it all the more painful? Seems it would be a constant reminder that she's gone."

I shook my head.

"Rob, do not tell me she is gone! As long as the seasons work their artful change on the ancient trees growing on the hills of Kentucky; as long as cold water gurgles over slate-bottomed creeks; as long as I have breath in my body—she is not gone!"

Oh, Bett, I love you
and I promise . . .
  I shall walk the hills with you.

9:35 P.M.

"Ginilou, can we talk a bit about Jolie?"

"Sure, tell me about Jolie, Rob."

"I've already told you some things, like how I feel when I'm with her. The problem isn't when I'm with her. It's when I'm *not* with her."

"You told me that Jolie is perfect, and you've made it clear that she cares for you. Now there's a problem?"

"Well, sometimes I begin to wonder just how she'll fit into my life if we aren't just two, but one! I wonder . . . oh, just forget it! I can't verbalize this. It isn't important anyway." He quickly turned away from me and gazed sullenly into space.

"Obviously, Rob, it *is* important. Tell me about it?"

"I really don't know." He turned toward me as he spoke. "I suppose it's just that Jolie is free. She mostly does what she wishes. She walks or runs where and when the mood hits. She isn't hampered by protocol or what is accepted behavior. If she wanted to run barefoot through the grass in front of City Hall at high noon, or at midnight, she'd do it.

"Don't get me wrong, I appreciate her exuberance for life, truly I do. Even if I don't completely understand it. In fact, to tell you the truth, it's really kind of exciting. But other people do not understand. Other people do not, would not, cannot accept her."

"Is that important to you?"

"I'm a respected attorney, believe it or not, and I . . . well, I have my friends . . . and—"

"And if Jolie were to be the wife of this 'most respected attorney,' she would have to fit whatever the mold is for accepted attorneys' wives. Is that what you're saying?"

"It would help," he said softly.

"Help who?"

"Me . . . us . . . it would help us."

"I see. Tell me this, Rob, was Beth acceptable to them?"

"Well, yes, she was."

"But Beth really wasn't acceptable to your needs at all."

"No."

"And if Jolie should give up her fascination with living and experiencing—if she traded her free laugh for a dainty smile, her wiggle-all-over-joy for a polite twinkle in the eye, her running barefoot and carefree through your life for sedate measured steps at your side—would she be 'Jolie' anymore?

"Or, perchance would she be a 'beth' who remotely somewhat resembles a once-upon-a-time-jolie?"

"Stop! Don't! ... don't ... please don't!"

"Rob, either a jolie is worth having, or she's not! Either a jolie makes a difference, or she doesn't! Either you want a jolie, or you don't! But don't you dare put it onto other things, other people, other considerations!

"Just what is a jolie worth on today's market to you?"

The answer came in well-measured tones, each word was as weighty as if it were carved with precision in blocks of marble: "Jolie is irreplaceable!"

"Right, Sir Idiot!"

"Ginilou, is it easy for you to say the words, 'I love you'?"

"No, not easy at all. I have great difficulty saying words that mean a lot to me, like 'friend.' 'special,' 'love.' I keep thinking our English language came up terribly short when it was decided to have such an important word cover fourteen square miles of territorial meaning.

"I know someone who occasionally uses the word 'friend' when what he really means is that he knows the person's name and can talk to him for three minutes without throwing up on his shoes!"

"Now that I think of it," Rob agreed, "I am afraid I do the very same thing. It's easy to say 'friend,' though most times I say it simply because if I don't, the other person will be offended."

"And the word 'love'?"

"Yeah, I've said that word when I really have felt quite guilty about using it. And then, there are times when I *should* have said it, times when I really felt it, but I just could not get the words out. Do you know, Ginilou, I can't even tell my dad I love him! Why is that? I do love him, I know I do. But I don't seem to be able to say it. And I know that it would mean a lot to him if I would. But when the time presents itself, I just feel awkward and say nothing."

Not long ago, I heard the very same problem expressed by someone half Rob's age.

As fingers of bright orange played along the ocean's edge he became caught up in a compulsion of sorts to share with me his feelings about the person who meant more to him than any other—his dad.

"My dad," he said, so proud of this man who fathered him.

"My dad!" His eyes sparkled and flashed, then suddenly grew somber and sad and filled with tears, as words too weighty spilled from his mouth and into my silent hands.

"My dad!" he said as he tilted his head to one side, a frown slithering across his forehead— spoke in soft, hesitant tones.

"My dad . . ." He threw back his head and shook the hair from his eyes. Laughter swelled from deep within, and his words were free and fast and joyous.

"My dad . . ." He stared at his shoes—his mouth becoming a hard line, his nostrils flaring, and he appeared not to be breathing at all as the words came clipped from between clenched teeth—angry words, painful words.

"My dad . . ." He hunched his shoulders forward and shivered. His eyes closed. There were no more words, and only his leaning toward me told me that he knew I was still there.

Later, the jauntiness began to reassert itself and he looked deep into my eyes. For an instant, once more temporarily stilled by seriousness, he slowly raised his hand and touched my lips with his fingertips. He smiled a gentle, easy smile and nodded his head. He understood his words were safe.

"Do you?" I asked him. "Do you love your dad?"

"Yes . . . oh, yes. He's my dad, and you know I love him."

"Then tell him."

"I can't . . . oh, I can't. I don't know how."

The flight attendant brought us each a cup of coffee and Rob took a couple of sips before he continued.

"Sometimes when I've visited with Dad and it's time to leave I find myself aching to say, 'I love you.' But all it seems I can do is to hug him tight and hope that he'll feel it flowing through me. And then, sometimes, I find myself just wanting to yell out, 'Dad, look at me! Really look at me! Tell me that you love me.'

"I know that he loves me. He would have had to, or else he couldn't have done all that he's done for Joe and me. But still, I do wish he could just say it. I've waited all these years and I've never heard him say the words. He's patted my shoulder, provided clothes and shelter and money for education, but he has never said the words.

"Perhaps if he had been able to put his love into words as well as action, Joey and I wouldn't find it equally difficult to do so now," Rob stated sadly. I nodded in understanding.

"In our family we've always been able to say 'I love you' to each other," I told him. "We've been lucky that way. Once, not so long ago, someone told me that if he heard the words 'I love you' all the time it would be commonplace, sort of like having steak every day. Well, I don't know about having steak every day, I've never had the chance to try that. But I *can* tell you that for me, no matter how often I'd hear it, 'I love you' would *never* become commonplace!

"When I was tadpole-sized, I overheard my father in conversation with a group of his fellow ministers. They were discussing death, and my dad said that when his time should come to 'shuffle off this mortal coil,' he hoped it would be on a Sunday morning after he had just preached. His companions were impressed, and I could see them saying to themselves, 'Wish I'd said that.' However, I can tell you that no matter how pleased they were, it scared me to death! To this day I carry with me a vague distrust of Sunday morning services!

"I even began having nightmares where I'd see Dad standing behind the pulpit preaching and then he would stop and say, 'I can no longer stand,' and then he'd sink down behind the pulpit. In my dream no matter how hard I tried to get to him it was impossible, my feet were glued to the floor!

"Years after I had left the tadpole stage far behind, I visited a large Detroit church where Dad was to preach one Sunday morning. The service had been an enjoyable worship experience and Dad's sermon was drawing to a close. I was, at the moment, entranced by the shifting patterns of light on the chancel carpet caused by the sun filtering through the red stained-glass windows. From afar off I heard the words that sent me plunging and spinning backwards straight into the middle of my childhood nightmare: 'Ladies and gentlemen, I am too weak to stand.' Before our eyes, Dad disappeared behind the pulpit. The congregation stood to be dismissed by the associate pastor, assuming that Dad had simply sat down, but I knew differently.

"There was no easy way to get to him, but I *had* to get to him. You could not have stopped me with mere convention—or with a Sherman tank. Over the tops of the pews I went—miniskirt, spiked heels, and all! Up through the chancel to Daddy's side. I knelt there, opened his robe, cradled his head in my hands, and with tears streaming down my face, I said over and over again, 'I love you, Daddy, I love you.'

"He opened his fever-closed eyes. Perspiration was beaded against his chalk-white face. He tried to smile. His eyes fluttered shut. Finally, out of trembly lips, seeped the whispered words, 'I love you.'

"Now, I've told this story before and almost

always people miss the point. You see, while it was extremely important for me to get to my dad, for me to say and hear him say, 'I love you,' it was no more important or meaningful then than it was today when I walked through his house and he was on his way out to feed the dog: 'Dad, I love you,' 'I love you, honey.'

"You see? Love is *always* important!"

"Yeah, I know. I do know," Rob said. "I only wish that I could do that. You know, there must be a secret to it, some easy way to learn, something that can free a person from the jitters inside and let the words out."

"I don't know what the secret would be, unless it's just to mean the words. Often we're stopped from saying what we feel. Before we open our mouths we start tacking on little why not reasons. A person may think, *If I say 'I love you' to my dad, he'll think I've gone soft in the head—that I'm a sissy! If I say 'I love you' to her—then she'll expect more from me!* Reckon we just should mean: 'I love you.' That should be easy to do. It should be!"

I love you!
    It's not easy to say.
    But I *can* tell you,
        if only you want to hear it!
    I can tell you.
I love you!
        and my insides do not
        shrivel up and shudder
        as if I had just swallowed
        a dose of castor oil!

See? Look! I love you!
   and saying it
   makes my eyes sparkle
   and my knees smile
   and my toes giggle.
Hey! I love you!
   Are you grinning?
   Are you smiling?
   Are you leaping with delight
     and spinning 'round 'n 'round
     and running through fields of clover
      to stand atop a knoll and shout
      to the heavens
"She loves me!"
Oh, I hope so, friend!
For I will be that ecstatic (and more)
if you say,
"I love you!"

9:40 P.M.

"Ginilou, earlier we were talking about images and I'm a little curious. Has your image of me changed during this flight because of all the in-depth talking we've been doing?"

"Changed? No, not 'changed.' You have, however, added considerably to my first impression of you."

Rob smiled. "When I first boarded," he said, "and saw you staring so intently out the window, I thought, 'I'm glad they assigned me this seat. I'm so tired and she is so preoccupied with something that she'll not bother me at all.' " Rob chuckled, "I'm still glad that they assigned me this seat, but the reason has changed."

"Are you gonna tell me the reason, Rob?"

"No."

"You sound like someone I know who never seems to tell me the answers to the questions he inspires—questions that nibble at the edges of me and jostle about in my brain!"

"Ginilou, is he a special person to you?"

"Yes."

"Tell me about him?"

"No."

As Rob's laugh faded he said, "Ginilou, you are very self-sufficient!"

"No. I am not."

"No? My goodness, that surprises me! I'd have been willing to bet that you could handle any-thing."

"You'd have been wrong."

"Now, my dear, I am more than a little curious. Just what is it that you can't handle?"

"What can't I handle well? A press of people where I cannot see each pair of eyes. Once there was a man, his face hidden by a ski mask. His face I couldn't recognize, but I will know those eyes if I ever see them again.

"What can't I handle well? People talking loudly all at once so that I cannot be aware of a particular deep voice that clips its words. *That* voice I will recognize if ever I hear it again.

"What can't I handle well?

Remembering

being

raped.

"The Rams were playing the Lions and I wanted to hear the next play, but it was time to take the cake out of the oven. So I turned the television volume up loud and reluctantly went to rescue my cake.

"Then the telephone rang. It was Mrs. Robb again and as I sat down to listen while she told me of her lonely day, my cat, Mouse, jumped up on the telephone table—which wasn't like him at all. Before I could brush him off the tabletop, he jumped down and spat at my feet. He scratched my toes, pushed his head against my knee, and tried in every way to get me out of the chair. Increasingly exasperated by his actions and finally having soothed Mrs. Robb, I placed the receiver back on the hook, intending to put that cat outside and turn down the volume on the television.

"As I stood up and turned something hit me, hard, across the cheekbone. I fell backward and landed in the hallway. I shook my head to clear it, and when I looked up, there stood a man, dressed in black, wearing a ski mask and holding a pistol.

"What can't I handle well? Remembering the barrel of the pistol striking my cheekbone again and again. Being tied. Being used. Being sick and feeling the blood run down my face. Sensing the scream rising from inside me as he laughed and shaved the hair from my scalp.

"What can't I handle well? A man touching me."

Silence was followed by silence. Then softly, emotionally, Rob spoke, "I am so sorry, so very sorry. Dear Ginilou, you have so much love inside of you to give. You're warm and open—and with the right man it will be right. It will! And he will help you to forget."

"Yes, I know. He will try, but, Rob, there are some things one never totally forgets—some things too big for life's eraser to handle."

"Ginilou?" In the growing silence, Rob touched my arm. "Would you please answer some questions for me? I'm not meaning simply to be inquisitive. I can see that it's painful for you. But it would help me in my work—and just maybe allow me to be that hand up to someone who needs it. Please?"

"What do you want to know?"

"Did you fight him?"

"Rob, I did everything! I tried everything I'd ever heard of, everything I'd ever read. But all of my reading of actual case histories, of psychology, of fiction—*all* were useless!

"It's so easy to know exactly what you'd do in any situation, until you're in that situation. I always knew what I'd do in the situation where a husband drank too much—until he did! I always knew what I'd do in the situation where a husband was compulsively unfaithful—until he was!

"I always knew what I'd do if a man was attempting to rape me—until it happened!

"Then, I found out that all the answers haven't been given yet, 'cause all the questions haven't been asked."

"What advise can you give women?"

"Wish I could give you a solution, but I can't. I don't know of one, or else I would have used it! Some things work in some situations, but in other situations nothing works."

"And afterward? What about afterward?"

"Rob, I only know the afterward for me. Afterward . . . I did not talk. I thought words, and it came as quite a shock to realize that somehow the passageway from thought words to audible words was disconnected. My mouth could open, but there was no way to get the words into the area where they might be heard. I tried. I did try. And then I was too tired to try anymore. My head hurt—I couldn't see out of my swollen right eye, my body ached, my scalp felt bruised and burned."

"And your God, Ginilou, where was he? Didn't he help?"

"Oh, Rob, when will you learn about my relationship to God? God doesn't just magically appear at 7:00 in the morning and at 11:30 at night to have a little 'chat' and pick up his praises. He's there all the time, not just when the world falls in.

"Communication with God, for me, has no formal beginning, no definite end. It's ongoing, it's 'Oh, and by the way . . .'

"I don't remember the two-hour drive from my house to my parents' home. They opened the door, and the shock on their faces surprised me (it never occurred to me that they didn't know all that had happened).

"Daddy helped me up the stairs. Mother helped me into the shower. For some reason the water beating upon my body, all bruised and bleeding, reminded me of BB pellets from a Daisy pistol striking against a cardboard target when I was four years old and Daddy taught me to aim and shoot.

"Then, somehow, miraculously, I was in a warm, sweet-smelling bed—my throbbing head cushioned in a soft pillow, Mother doctoring my bleeding cheek, Daddy rubbing my cramping legs, the girls putting lotion on my rope-marked wrists and watching with big eyes, filled to overflowing with love and tears.

"And finally—mercifully—Someone let drowsiness fog my burning brain and weariness creep up my body to dull the ache and ease me into healing sleep."

"Ah, Ginilou, when all you know are the facts on a police blotter—just facts, black and white, stark and unfeeling—you don't know all the rest, all the immeasurable damage. You can't understand the total picture. But I make this promise to you—I will *never* again joke about rape. And I will, to the best of my ability, be sensitive and speak softly, soothingly, and lovingly to the rape victims who come to me for legal assistance. I promise!"

"Some things people just never understand—rape is one of them. There are times when I've heard someone start to tell those jokes. You know the ones, 'No one could ever rape my wife, she'd be too willing. Ha-ha-ha-ha.' And I could scream. But I don't. I sit there, quietly, while the blood pounds in my ears and I remember. It's not one of those things easily talked about. Besides my parents, children, and closest friend, I have only talked of it to two others—both of them rape victims. Now, I have told you, and if it helps you to be of comfort and help to someone else, then it was worth the telling."

"Ginilou, you know, some people who have known me for years and who even think of themselves as my close friends would find it difficult to understand that right now you probably know me better than they do."

"Knowing a person isn't really a matter of time. Most of the time all of us try to keep people from knowing the real person we are inside."

"You, too?"

"Sure. I'm not really a very trusting person, like I've already told you. Most of the time the real me just sits inside and lets the majority of people think that whatever they see, whatever they choose to believe, is me. Sometimes that person is a part of me, and sometimes she isn't. There are really very few people that I allow to know me."

"How does a person really get to know someone? It's important to me that I really know Jolie, and that she know me."

"Are you sure?"

"Yes, I am!"

"Be very sure, Rob. Once upon a time, in a day long ago, the person who is now my closest friend said to me, 'Will you be my friend? I want to be your friend. Please, help me to know you.' And I looked into his eyes and suddenly felt very exhausted with all the pretense and the games people play to keep one another out. I wanted a friend—someone who would care—someone who could know the real me and still not cringe or walk away. So, taking a deep breath, I said yes. I don't regret that decision, but I must admit it hasn't always been easy. There have been times when I'd rather have avoided some questions or not have been completely truthful. You know, just told part of the truth and left the rest unsaid. But I promised to help him to know me! It takes work to know someone, it takes work to allow yourself to be known. You have to allow yourself to be trusting, to let down the walls, and risk becoming vulnerable. You have to be willing to extend yourself, to guard the privilege of being close, to provide the time it takes to communicate."

"But isn't it worth it?"

"When it's right, it's worth everything."

"Ginilou, I wish I knew you."

"Knowing isn't done by wishing, knowing is done by doing."

Arrival Time—Nashville
9:55 P.M.

"I can honestly say I've never had such a concentrated period or indepth talk with anyone before in my entire life! Oh, I've been engaged in conversation with people for more than four hours before, but *never* anything like this. Never have I felt so drained, so stripped of pretense, so vulnerable somehow. Maybe an open wound feels like this."

"Sorry, Rob."

"Don't be! Now that the wounds are open, I believe there is a chance for healing."

"Oh, Rob! Look at those beautiful lights below us! That must be Nashville—look how beautiful!"

"Looks like a giant Christmas tree!"

"Have you ever seen anything so beautiful? I mean, have you ever seen anything like this, more beautiful than this?"

"Never! Say, are you going to tell me that God lit all those beautiful lights just for us to enjoy?"

Rob asked me with a twinkle in his eyes.

"No, I am not, High and Noble Sarcastic Person!"

His laugh floated comfortably and intimately between us. "Oh, my dear Ginilou, whoever is responsible for lighting those lights, I am most happy that he is allowing them to share their beauty with you."

"Thank you, kind sir."

"Won't be long now till we're on the ground. The way you're touching your ears again, I'd say it's time for you to start swallowing."

"Seems like we're going to end this night flight just the same way we started it."

"How can that be? I'm not the same person I was when this flight began. It can't end the same. Definitely not."

"Funny, you look the same to me."

"Well, I'm not the same. Sometime during the stop at Birmingham, I noted that I apparently had misplaced a lot of the anger that I've carried with me for years. While I cannot forgive my mother as yet, I can, on the other hand, admit that I remember she taught me some positive things when I was a child. Maybe that's why they are a part of my personality today. Maybe! So, just maybe, I can start saying 'I don't understand' why she left us, instead of 'I hate her for leaving.'

"And something else, a whole new dimension has been added to my life. The concept of a hand up and paying up for being a member of the family of man.

"Then there is Jolie. Listen to me say it . . . I love Jolie. How about *that!*

"What a marvelous journey this has been—all the way from who I was to who I am becoming. No, most assuredly I am not the same person I was four hours ago!

"Ginilou, I do wish you well on your book. What an exciting period this will be in your life!"

"Oh, I hope so! I'm looking forward to it. Reckon I could do with a dab of 'exciting.' And I wish you well on this most joyous phase of your life. For everything there is a season and for every matter under heaven—a time to weep; a time to laugh, mourn, dance. Oh, Rob! In your life, this is the time to love!"

"A time to love," Rob mused. "A time to love, that *is* exciting. And, Ginilou, I vow I shall start now!"

The flight attendant's voice came crisply over the intercom, "All persons terminating their flight with us in Nashville are to come forward as we come to a stop. Have a good stay in Nashville and fly with us again soon. Those of you continuing on to Washington and New York, please remain seated. We'll be taking off in fifteen minutes."

"Well, guess this is good-bye, Rob."

"Wait, I'll walk with you into the terminal."

"The flight attendant said to stay seated."

"I know, but you said I was used to handling people! Watch me!"

After speaking to the flight attendant, Rob walked with me into the travel way that led into the airport. We walked along in silence. At the connecting doorway he turned to me and paused.

"I'll leave you here. I find it almost impossible, but still I know that it's true. Ginilou, I am going to miss you."

He put his arm around my shoulder and gently kissed me good-bye.

"By the way, you *are* earthy!"

"Well, spread the word!"

"Earthy and crazy! Wait! Before you walk through that door, I have to know—in a world where most people are takers and not givers, have you shed a great many tears because of looking with eyes of love?"

"Oh, Rob, crying is one of my better talents! I do it well!

> But mostly my tears have been because
>> I was misunderstood,
>> not trusted,
>> not wanted.
> I have to believe that love is the most
>> important thing!
>> If there be tears,
>> let them be because of
>>> words not spoken,
>>> dreams not dreamed,
>>> laughter not shared,
>>> warmth not kindled.
>> But most of all,
>> if there be tears,
>> let them be because of
>>> love not given."

"I'll remember that. And Ginilou, when you get around to writing about this, you have my permission! Just please don't you dare make me look like too much of an idiot!"

We laughed comfortably at the idea, and he opened the door for me.

"One last thing, Earthy Person. When *he* gets around to telling *you* that he loves you, will you be listening?"

"Ah, Rob . . . that's why I grew ears!"

The door eased shut. I turned, took a deep breath, straightened my shoulders: "Oh, Nashville, here's the new kid on the block!"

Epilogue

There are clothes to wash and suitcases to unpack. After ten days on the road, smiling and shaking hands, autographing books, and giving concerts, it is so good to be back home. Still, there are clothes to wash, furniture to dust, plants to touch, feed, and water, dog ears to pet—yet here I sit . . . just breathing!

Brrring!
Brrring!
Brrring!

(I had almost forgotten there were telephones to answer!)

"Hello?"

"Hello, Earthy!"

"Rob!"

"You remembered, aw, shucks! How nice!"

"Well, some people are worth remembering, and some you remember just by accident in spite of yourself!"

"Oh, thanks heaps! And do you remember, by accident of course, that it has been almost exactly one year since we took a night flight together?"

"I *do* remember!"

"Guess what happened to me two weeks ago!"

"You got run over by a herd of rabid elephants."

"Uhhhh, no . . . but you're close! Two weeks ago I was in Denver waiting for a limo to take me from the hotel to the airport. While I paced back and forth impatiently I happened to glance in a bookstore window and there you were on a book cover! I couldn't have been more surprised! I rushed in, grabbed the book, paid for it, and read it on the flight back home."

"What did you think of it—the book, not the flight?"

"It's just like you—the book, not the flight."

"I don't know whether that's a compliment or not!"

"Well, I've ordered ten!"

"Bless your gizzard, you sweet man!"

"Are you writing another?"

"As a matter of fact, yes, I am! Actually it concerns our flight together last year."

"You're kidding! What's the title?"

"No, I am not kidding! After all, you already gave me permission to do so! And the title is *The Most Important Thing.*"

"Good title. I like it. That's exactly what it was . . . what it is . . . and shall forever be! Listen, you didn't make me into a complete idiot, did you?"

"Only when you were! Tell me, Rob. How *are* you?"

"Fantastic! This past year has been good, very good! I'm learning and growing, and I think I've become more sensitive to people's needs. And I certainly am enjoying life more than I ever dreamed possible."

"And Jolie?"

His laugh was as I remembered it, warm and infectious. "Jolie is, as always, magnificent. Our relationship is one of the great positives of life. Of course, now and then, there are other things that may be not so—oh, I'm not sure what I'm trying to say. It's . . ."

"Even though the things surrounding the two of you may not always be perfect, the two of you together are good—indestructible—constant!"

"Yes. Exactly! And I have made a discovery this past year. When living with an eye toward chances to be a hand up, and when looking seriously for opportunities to pay your dues, one is so busy looking outward that he forgets to worry so much about being vulnerable. And a most wondrous thing happens, the person-to-God love relationship, and the person-to-person love relationship flow together into a most magnificent zest for living!"

"You discovered that, huh?"

"Yep, you sarcastic person, I did! And I must also tell you that hanging on the wall behind my desk is a saying that I had an artist friend of mine (Jolie, to be exact) script and frame for me. I look at it every day. It says:

'Love
is the most important thing there is!
   'n if there be tears . . .
   let them be for the times you
   walked on by
   and didn't recognize the time to love!' "

We chatted comfortably for a bit, shared a
laugh or two, and promised to keep in touch.
   "Ginilou, tell me again, is love *still* the most
important thing?"
   "Love is, forever, the most important thing."

Tonight I sit here on the dock. The evening is
still and warm, the lake calm.
   Surrounding me are strange, opposing
feelings of
      sadness and hope,
      apprehension and excitement.
   My thoughts skitter about
      as fast as the minnows
      at the lake's edge.
   I am grateful
      for family,
      love, closeness,
      friendship,
      and the chance to contribute!
   And the
      bittersweet melodies
      that beckon me on
      . . . to what
         I do not know.
   "O Lord, fill me with love!"

"Hey, what'cha got in your basket, little girl?"
"Oh, I gots me flowers. Loverly spring flowers,
    'n three kisses
    six smiles
    two belly laughs
    five cuddles
    one lil' package of hope
    two teensy dreams
    four fluffy desires
    one piece of string
    one whistle
    three lil' words
    a tiny green rain-frog
    'n a jar of sweet honey!
"That's what I got in my basket!"
"Hey, little girl, will you let me see?"
"No, they's *mine!*"
  Along life's journey
    if there be tears,
    let them be for
    'let me see's'
      not shared!

Other Living Books Best-sellers

THE ANGEL OF HIS PRESENCE by Grace Livingston Hill. This book captures the romance of John Wentworth Stanley and a beautiful young woman whose influence causes John to reevaluate his well-laid plans for the future. 07-0047 $2.95.

ANSWERS by Josh McDowell and Don Stewart. In a question-and-answer format, the authors tackle sixty-five of the most-asked questions about the Bible, God, Jesus Christ, miracles, other religions, and creation. 07-0021 $3.95.

THE BEST CHRISTMAS PAGEANT EVER by Barbara Robinson. A delightfully wild and funny story about what happens to a Christmas program when the "Horrible Herdman" brothers and sisters are miscast in the roles of the biblical Christmas story characters. 07-0137 $2.50.

BUILDING YOUR SELF-IMAGE by Josh McDowell. Here are practical answers to help you overcome your fears, anxieties, and lack of self-confidence. Learn how God's higher image of who you are can take root in your heart and mind. 07-1395 $3.95.

THE CHILD WITHIN by Mari Hanes. The author shares insights she gained from God's Word during her own pregnancy. She identifies areas of stress, offers concrete data about the birth process, and points to God's sure promises that he will "gently lead those that are with young." 07-0219 $2.95.

COME BEFORE WINTER AND SHARE MY HOPE by Charles R. Swindoll. A collection of brief vignettes offering hope and the assurance that adversity and despair are temporary setbacks we can overcome! 07-0477 $5.95.

DARE TO DISCIPLINE by James Dobson. A straightforward, plainly written discussion about building and maintaining parent/child relationships based upon love, respect, authority, and ultimate loyalty to God. 07-0522 $3.50.

DAVID AND BATHSHEBA by Roberta Kells Dorr. This novel combines solid biblical and historical research with suspenseful storytelling about men and women locked in the eternal struggle for power, governed by appetites they wrestle to control. 07-0618 $4.95.

FOR MEN ONLY edited by J. Allan Petersen. This book deals with topics of concern to every man: the business world, marriage, fathering, spiritual goals, and problems of living as a Christian in a secular world. 07-0892 $3.95.

FOR WOMEN ONLY by Evelyn and J. Allan Petersen. Balanced, entertaining, diversified treatment of all the aspects of womanhood. 07-0897 $4.95.

400 WAYS TO SAY I LOVE YOU by Alice Chapin. Perhaps the flame of love has almost died in your marriage. Maybe you have a good marriage that just needs a little "spark." Here is a book especially for the woman who wants to rekindle the flame of romance in her marriage; who wants creative, practical, useful ideas to show the man in her life that she cares. 07-0919 $2.95.

Other Living Books Best-sellers

GIVERS, TAKERS, AND OTHER KINDS OF LOVERS by Josh McDowell and Paul Lewis. This book bypasses vague generalities about love and sex and gets right to the basic questions: Whatever happened to sexual freedom? What's true love like? Do men respond differently than women? If you're looking for straight answers about God's plan for love and sexuality, this book was written for you. 07-1031 $2.95.

HINDS' FEET ON HIGH PLACES by Hannah Hurnard. A classic allegory of a journey toward faith that has sold more than a million copies! 07-1429 $3.95.

HOW TO BE HAPPY THOUGH MARRIED by Tim LaHaye. One of America's most successful marriage counselors gives practical, proven advice for marital happiness. 07-1499 $3.50.

JOHN, SON OF THUNDER by Ellen Gunderson Traylor. In this saga of adventure, romance, and discovery, travel with John — the disciple whom Jesus loved — down desert paths, through the courts of the Holy City, to the foot of the cross. Journey with him from his luxury as a privileged son of Israel to the bitter hardship of his exile on Patmos. 07-1903 $4.95.

LIFE IS TREMENDOUS! by Charlie "Tremendous" Jones. Believing that enthusiasm makes the difference, Jones shows how anyone can be happy, involved, relevant, productive, healthy, and secure in the midst of a high-pressure, commercialized society. 07-2184 $2.95.

LOOKING FOR LOVE IN ALL THE WRONG PLACES by Joe White. Using wisdom gained from many talks with young people, White steers teens in the right direction to find love and fulfillment in a personal relationship with God. 07-3825 $3.95.

LORD, COULD YOU HURRY A LITTLE? by Ruth Harms Calkin. These prayer-poems from the heart of a godly woman trace the inner workings of the heart, following the rhythms of the day and the seasons of the year with expectation and love. 07-3816 $2.95.

LORD, I KEEP RUNNING BACK TO YOU by Ruth Harms Calkin. In prayer-poems tinged with wonder, joy, humanness, and questioning, the author speaks for all of us who are groping and learning together what it means to be God's child. 07-3819 $3.50.

MORE THAN A CARPENTER by Josh McDowell. A hard-hitting book for people who are skeptical about Jesus' deity, his resurrection, and his claims on their lives. 07-4552 $2.95.

MOUNTAINS OF SPICES by Hannah Hurnard. Here is an allegory comparing the nine spices mentioned in the Song of Solomon to the nine fruits of the Spirit. A story of the glory of surrender by the author of *HINDS' FEET ON HIGH PLACES*. 07-4611 $3.95.

NOW IS YOUR TIME TO WIN by Dave Dean. In this true-life story, Dean shares how he locked into seven principles that enabled him to bounce back from failure to success. Read about successful men and women — from sports and entertainment celebrities to the ordinary people next door — and discover how you too can bounce back from failure to success! 07-4727 $2.95.

Other Living Books Best-sellers

THE POSITIVE POWER OF JESUS CHRIST by Norman Vincent Peale. All his life the author has been leading men and women to Jesus Christ. In this book he tells of his boyhood encounters with Jesus and of his spiritual growth as he attended seminary and began his world-renowned ministry. 07-4914 $4.50.

REASONS by Josh McDowell and Don Stewart. In a convenient question-and-answer format, the authors address many of the commonly asked questions about the Bible and evolution. 07-5287 $3.95.

ROCK by Bob Larson. A well-researched and penetrating look at today's rock music and rock performers, their lyrics, and their life-styles. 07-5686 $3.50.

THE STORY FROM THE BOOK. The full sweep of *The Book's* content in abridged, chronological form, giving the reader the "big picture" of the Bible. 07-6677 $4.95.

SUCCESS: THE GLENN BLAND METHOD by Glenn Bland. The author shows how to set goals and make plans that really work. His ingredients of success include spiritual, financial, educational, and recreational balances. 07-6689 $3.50.

TELL ME AGAIN, LORD, I FORGET by Ruth Harms Calkin. You will easily identify with the author in this collection of prayer-poems about the challenges, peaks, and quiet moments of each day. 07-6990 $3.50.

THROUGH GATES OF SPLENDOR by Elisabeth Elliot. This unforgettable story of five men who braved the Auca Indians has become one of the most famous missionary books of all times. 07-7151 $3.95.

WAY BACK IN THE HILLS by James C. Hefley. The story of Hefley's colorful childhood in the Ozarks makes reflective reading for those who like a nostalgic journey into the past. 07-7821 $4.50.

WHAT WIVES WISH THEIR HUSBANDS KNEW ABOUT WOMEN by James Dobson. The best-selling author of *DARE TO DISCIPLINE* and *THE STRONG-WILLED CHILD* brings us this vital book that speaks to the unique emotional needs and aspirations of today's woman. An immensely practical, interesting guide. 07-7896 $3.50.

The books listed are available at your bookstore. If unavailable, send check with order to cover retail price plus $1.00 per book for postage and handling to:

Tyndale DMS
Box 80
Wheaton, Illinois 60189

Prices and availability subject to change without notice. Allow 4–6 weeks for delivery.